Praise for *The Wizard of Oz Code*:

"*The Wizard of Oz Code* takes us through a journey of going within to garner the courage to open our hearts and overcome our fears. The journey down the Yellow Brick Road encourages us to explore our Physical, Mental, Spiritual and Emotional Expressions, finding the way to happiness; skipping through life, no matter what fears or obstacles show up along the way. *The Wizard of Oz Code* Journal suggestions and practical tools, given throughout the book, offer us the Courage and Strength to open our hearts with Love while on this amazing journey to Oz."
- Cynde Meyer, publisher of Spirit Seeker Magazine, and Intuitive Life Coach

"Mich Hancock brings forth an inspiring life changing read as she brilliantly unlocks the hidden symbols of *The Wizard of Oz*. We find ourselves traveling the transformational yellow brick road; gathering personal insight and wisdom. As our heroes meet challenges they grow, mature and heal. Prepare to enter the world "Over the Rainbow" where you will find the miraculous realm of healing and transformation. Your perception of life will change forever."
-Donna Nicks RPT, www.breath-of-heaven.com

"In *The Wizard of Oz Code*, Mich Hancock does a masterful job of examining this classic story and uncovering the timeless lessons hidden within. Read this book and discover why Dorothy's journey down the Yellow Brick Road holds so much wisdom. A real gem!"
-Bob Baker, author of *Unleash the Artist Within* and *Guerrilla Music Marketing Handbook*, www.bob-baker.com

And More Praise . . . .

"Mich has very insightfully interwoven the metaphors of a classic movie into a guide for expansion of self awareness, spiritual and emotional growth. The timing of Mich's book is so synchronistic, due to the many souls that are currently on Earth and are seeking more joy, love and meaning in their lives. There is something for everyone in *The Wizard of Oz Code*. Whether you are a veteran or just starting your journey of enlightenment and expansion, you will find guidance in this wonderful book."
-Barbara Becherer, LPC, RPT-S, NCC, NCCH

"How Mich decoded *The Wizard of Oz* is otherworldly! As I poured over the pages, the code was crystal clear, made sense and was easily applicable to anyone's personal journey of self-discovery and becoming. By the end, the reader has been equipped with a simple means to get "over their rainbow." Mich takes us on a scene-by-scene journey through an awakening into our Divine Selves and Potential. Each scene is brought to light through an "obvious" awareness, and then made applicable through the great and powerful perspectives. All is then wrapped neatly with a bow, via the exercises that simplify and support the readers' journey down their own yellow brick road to Oz; and finally to the sweet spot where Mich has newly defined that *there's no place like home!*"
- Simone Peer, PCC, PMC

The Wizard of Oz Code

Mich Hancock

Cover Design by Rob Jansen Graphics, St. Louis, MO
(Thank you, Dad!)

The Wizard of Oz Code

Published by LayaLuna, LLC
Hillsboro, MO USA

ISBN-10: 0-6153686-7-0
ISBN-13: 978-0-6153686-7-2

Printed in the United States of America

Disclaimer

The author of this book does not dispense medical advice, or prescribe the use of any technique as a form of treatment for physical, emotional, or medical problems without the advice of a physician, either directly or indirectly. The intent of the author is only to offer information of a general nature to help you in your quest for your emotional and spiritual well–being. In the event that you decide to use any of the information in this book for yourself, which is your constitutional right, the author and publisher assume no responsibility for your actions or outcome.

This book is neither endorsed nor authorized by Turner Entertainment Co.

Acknowledgments

This book could not have possibly been written without the guidance, support and love of my beautiful family and friends. I especially wish to say THANK YOU to:

My husband Dan, for growing up with me, believing in me and making it possible for me to stay at home and write. And for reading every single word again and again and again until I thought it was just right.

My son, James, for seeking out all that was hidden from me and creating a high necessity to heal everything, on every level.

My daughter Jordan, for bringing forth amazing wisdom, insight and strength and for reminding me to do the same – even when I didn't think I could go one step further.

My parents, Camilla and Rob, who brought me forth onto this earth, allowed me to grow into my authenticity and who tirelessly bring me respite, time and time again when my son is at his most challenging.

My brothers, Chris and Matt, for going on this wacky and wild life ride with me, and for accepting me as their sister; through all the changes and growth.

My husband's family; Deanna, Rod, David, Lynne and their families – for accepting this quirky in-law into your lives. And especially to Deanna and Rod for taking my son on a two week vacation so I could learn to breathe again.

Cynde Meyer, for being an amazing teacher, healer, on-earth guide, cheerleader, supporter, mentor and for lovingly challenging me to grow and expand.

Bob Baker for mentoring me in the world of self-publishing and for telling me that I could, in fact, make this book happen.

Barbara Becherer for her constant support, love and friendship. For her insights that go beyond this world. And for being so darn excited each time we discussed this book.

Cathy Barnett for hanging in there as a friend. From the high school pom pon squad to college to marriage and motherhood of disordered children, as well as painful losses, we have seen each other through many a storm.

Donna Nicks for guiding me to see my purpose and my path, and for helping me to accept the seemingly crazy going-ons and find the truth within.

Simone Peer for reading this entire book and sharing her editing skills and sage advice – thank you for helping me to make this book into a polished final product. And for being an amazing friend.

Sheridan Stiarwalt for her loving friendship and calming influence in this chaotic world. And for always calling me or emailing me exactly when I need to talk to her.

Judy Wolf for keeping myself and family in her thoughts and prayers and for sending healing energy to us in a most loving and giving manner.

Rich Lickel for being a kind, loving and giving energy in this world. And for offering support and a strong shoulder whenever and wherever needed.

Shirley Crenshaw for helping my family and I create some order in a highly disordered child.

Jeff Hartman for keeping me up on what is what when it comes to the web and patiently walking me through new technologies.

Waila Skinner for teaching me about web sites, advertising and marketing. And for designing my first web site (www.layaluna.com). She is amazing!

Rusti Levin, Spirit Seeker's amazing graphic design artist, who visits with me each month as we work together with Cynde Meyer to create the magazine. Pure love and energy goes into each issue.

My Personal Mastery Group – Judy, Sheridan, Rich, Sheryl, Mary, Cindy, Donna, and Lily Ann for supporting me through a time of super accelerated growth.

Carrie Anderson, who has explained to a whole lot of people in Hillsboro, Missouri, that I do not have cancer, but am simply a healthy gal sans hair. And for supporting me and believing me in my greatest time of need.

Sherrie Rodgers who keeps my house in pristine condition, helps me transport kids to/from school, brings me wonderful breads, teas and candles when I need to relax and returns my wayward dogs home when they go missing. We could not ask for a better neighbor and we love her and her children dearly.

The Clack Family for all their love and support. Truly one of the most unconditionally loving and close families I know – they have taught me many a lesson.

Angie Bregant for being a count on friend and always willing to lend an ear. And for being a particularly strong mother.

And to all the people who have allowed me to be a part of their healing and exploration into other existences.

About the Author:

Mich Hancock graduated with honors from St. Louis University, studying at both the St. Louis and Madrid, Spain campuses. She is certified in the Cannon Hypnosis Technique, a certified Holographic Sound Healer, Reiki Level II and Avesa Breath Practitioner.
She has trained in several forms of breathwork, meditation, and energy work.

Currently, she is a Writer, Music Reviewer and Editor for Spirit Seeker Magazine (www.spiritseeker.com). She has interviewed several top visionaries including Gregg Braden, Doreen Virtue, Marianne Williamson, Neale Donald Walsch, Gay Hendricks, and Dr. Masaru Emoto.

She lives in Hillsboro, Missouri with her husband, two children and two puppies.

Contents

Forward:

This book is for your own personal experience. It does not matter how you read this book or why you are reading it. Perhaps you are a huge fan of *The Wizard of Oz* and are interested in a new and entertaining view of this cherished classic. Perhaps you are awakening to your evolutionary journey and are looking for inspiration. It does not matter; for every reader, and for every way in which it is read, is perfect and in order.

It is perfect and in order because it is all in and of God, just as we are all in and of God. At the same time we are each a unique expression of God. On Earth this uniqueness is most apparent. So much so, that we feel and think we are separate from God, as well as from everything else. But we are not separate, in fact, we are quite connected; we are simply not aware of it. We do not even have an inkling that what we do affects people over on another continent, as well as the caterpillar clinging to the window, the grand tree in the Russian forest or the star in a galaxy far, far away.

Oneness is simply what *is*; we are each a part of God and All That Is. And we are being called to feel and know this connection. We are being called to realize that we are connected to every single speck and particle; here and into the far reaches of the Universe, as well as in the many dimensions, vibrations and frequencies.

It might seem an impossible concept to grasp. Oneness may sound all airy fairy, we-are-the-world, mumbo jumbo, feel good stuff. It feels this way because we don't really get it. And we don't get it because we do not feel or know our Soul. We have some loose ideas about our Soul and we are all pretty sure we have one. But where is it, how do we access it, how can we feel our connection to it?

The aim of this book is to help us to connect with our Souls and see beyond the illusion of separation. The veils of illusion are lifting right now, so why not be conscious of it and *get* what's going on? We are in the middle of our next human evolution and we are being called to awaken to Oneness. Feeling and knowing Oneness all starts with an inner journey that leads us to our Soul.

We have been provided with many hints about this awakening. Ancient cultures such as the Mayan and the Hopi provided us with *maps* to navigate these current times. But what if there is also a little bit more contemporary version of this map? I believe there is, and it can be found in *The Wizard of Oz*.

The Wizard of Oz points to the inner journey we can choose to take in order to understand what is going on in our own backyards. It is in Oz that we have the opportunity to redefine everything we know about ourselves and everything around us. It is a journey that leads us Home, to that part of us which is most realized in its connection to God, to our Soul, and to Oneness.

This inner journey is not the "righteous path" or the "moral way", but an ego-less, non-judgmental, and gracious road paved in truth, simplicity and love.

This road leads us to a wholeness of Self and Soul that can then be expressed as wholeness with All That Is. Within each of us is a cast of characters, each with a role, each with lessons and each providing an opportunity to mature, grow and expand.

Most specifically, we will follow along with the movie version of *The Wizard of Oz*, which so many of us have seen again and again, and with which so many of us have fallen in love. We love *The Wizard of Oz*, not only because it is a fascinating story, but because it is *Our Story*. It is the story of our current human evolution; where we transcend the limitations of Earth and live in an entirely new expression. It is a story rich with the language of our Soul; a language replete with imagery and symbolism. And our story is no less intriguing, adventurous, beautiful or amazing than that of Dorothy, the Scarecrow, the Cowardly Lion and the Tin Man.

About the Wizard of Oz Code

In order to truly begin to understand what we can do to reveal our Soul to ourselves and live in Oneness, we must change our limited perspectives. We must open ourselves up to a completely new way of being.

As we journey through *The Wizard of Oz* we will look at how each part of the story points to and provides us with clues on how we can bring awareness and change of perspective to our own lives. It is through awareness that we develop the ability to live from a more conscious place and see how we operate in this Earth life; thereby giving us the ability to question, learn, grow and understand why it is we do what we do. The change in perspective comes as we begin to see our lives from the much higher vantage point provided to us by our Soul.

In each section of our story we will take a scene from *The Wizard of Oz*. We will then look at that scene and see how it may presently be playing out in your own life, thereby providing you with an **Oz Awareness**. This is then followed by a **Great and Powerful Change in Perspective** that can help you begin to live life with a sight that emanates from Soul level.

It would be most beneficial for you to keep an **Oz Journal**. This journal is your travelogue; it helps you to see where you have been, where you are and, most importantly, where you can go. In it you can jot down your impressions about each scene and how it applies to your life, then how you can begin to change your perspective and live from a higher plane.

There are no rules, your Oz Journal reflects your own personal and unique journey, and you decide and choose your journey. Also, there is no time frame to adhere to. Allow yourself to unfold to changes and growth in a gentle and mindful manner that speaks to you. As you grow and bring new awareness and perspective into your life you will move from a contracted and diminished sense of self to an expansive existence.

And so I invite you to come with me as our story opens. Here we meet Dorothy and her dog Toto. The two are running away from Ms. Gulch, who as we find out later, is mighty peeved at Toto's garden antics and cat chasing ways.

1: Dorothy's Dilemma

Dorothy is off to let Uncle Henry and Auntie Em know just what is going on with the cranky Ms. Gulch. But when she arrives to the farm, Uncle Henry and Auntie Em have their own dilemma, they are too busy with an old incubator that has gone bad and are working frantically to save the baby chicks. They do not have time to listen to Dorothy's dilemma.

She then turns to the farmhands Zeke, Hunk and Hickory; who are quick with advice, though not exactly that of the helpful variety. Hunk, for example, suggests that she just quit going by Ms. Gulch's place; offering no alternative route. Zeke suggests that Dorothy simply spit in Ms. Gulch's eye. (Really, Zeke?)

Later in the scene, when Dorothy readdresses the issue with Auntie Em, Auntie Em tells her to "stop imagining things", to stop fretting "about nothing" and to find herself a place where she "won't get into any trouble."

Oz Awareness #1: Our Dilemmas

In our story, the word *dilemma* can be accurately described as *trauma*. We tend to view and handle our traumas in a similar sense. We diminish their impact upon our lives as a mere dilemma, when in actuality it is a trauma.

Sometimes our dilemma/traumas are handled by simply not handling them at all. Just as Dorothy does in the very beginning; she runs off to tell some body else about it, in the hope that they will fix it and make it all better. Other times we handle our dilemma/traumas by applying a quick pop-psychology band aid, as is provided to Dorothy via the farmhand's suggestions. Still, at other times we simply disregard the dilemma/trauma all together, as there are more *important* matters at hand. And this is shown to us through the words and actions of Auntie Em and Uncle Henry.

If we were to consider any of the aforementioned dilemma/trauma handlings, we would most likely find similar examples in our own life. Especially from childhood, when the adults in our lives told us that our dilemma/traumas were imagined, or that we were making too much of them or we need to just get over them as there are more significant things to consider.

To an adult, such childhood events can seem, well, childish. Our adult issues are way bigger and far more important than the simple cuts and scrapes of childhood. But what we fail to understand is that our big adult issues stem from a long ago dilemma/trauma that was ignored, or brushed over or answered with a pat on the head and a lollipop. The adults in our lives did not give the credence that our dilemma/traumas deserved. As a result, they remain with us.

And how the dilemma/trauma was handled, be them handled by the adults in our life at that time or by us as a child at the time (and left to our own devices), affects how we continue to handle them today. The way in which they were handled created an energetic pattern and this pattern will never go away until the original dilemma/trauma is released.

The energetic pattern will continue to play out in our lives, so much so that we actually come to resonate with and attract similar energy patterns. This affects everything from the types of companies we work for to the type of company we keep.

It is through these energetic patterns that we build habits, behaviors and addictions. Each time we engage in the habit, behavior or addiction, the energetic pattern becomes ever more ingrained. We literally condition ourselves to handle similar dilemma/traumas in much the same manner, over and over again.

As time goes on we come to forget how all of this started in the first place and we begin to say things like, "That's just the way I am" or "I have always been this way." We take on the energetic pattern as if it defines who we are. And if we do not release the original dilemma/traumas they continue to affect our lives and will grow to become ever more apparent.

As is the case with Dorothy, until she releases and heals, she will meet up with one Almira Gulch after another. Each Almira Gulch may look different, live in a different city and have a different name, but in Dorothy's future dilemma/traumas there is sure to be an Almira Gulch at its core. And it will become an ever more apparent part of her life, it will be as if Almira Gulch is following her and watching her every move.

We can continue to make the choice to ignore our dilemma/traumas. Or we can choose to see them for what they truly are, and for this we must be thankful.

Great and Powerful Perspective #1: Gratitude for Our Dilemmas

Consider some of the energetic patterns you have right now. Are you addicted to a substance, food or behavior? Do you have a tendency toward angry outbursts? Do you often fall into depression? Choose just one energetic pattern that you feel you are ready to take on today.

It is okay to start out small and test the waters; this energetic pattern need not be the *big one* just yet, go ahead and build up some momentum first. Then write about this energetic pattern in your Oz Journal.

Now see this for what it is, an energetic pattern; energy that has arranged itself into a pattern. Everything is energy. We forget this, but it is fact, everything can be brought down to an energetic level.

From the energy of the dilemma/trauma a pattern was created and this pattern is evident in your habits, behaviors and addictions. And we become so conditioned to it that we live with and from our energetic patterns in an unconscious manner. We can change this by replacing the energetic pattern that was unconsciously created, with one that is consciously created and vibrates at a higher level; this being the energetic pattern of Gratitude.

From here on out choose to be aware of when the energetic pattern is operating in your life, and rather than berate yourself, choose to be in a state of Gratitude.

This can be challenging, as we have not been conditioned to be thankful for that which brings us pain. Traditionally, we have viewed our energetic patterns from a state of *density*; density here meaning that we feel cut off from All That Is. And because we do not feel the connection with All That Is, we forget who we really are and why we are really here; we forget our truth.

However, we can begin to know our truth by choosing Gratitude for our energetic patterns. For within each energetic pattern lies the innate opportunity for growth and maturity. And it is for this, that we must be thankful.

This is why you are here. You chose to be here, on this Earth, so that you could grow and mature.

By dipping down into density, by creating *dilemma-ic responses* to your traumas, you set up your own educational program for amazing expansion.

Each time your conditioned energetic pattern starts up, be aware and be thankful. By doing so you are opening up to a new, more loving energy that will allow you to begin to change the pattern for your higher good.

It may help for you to first spend some time sensing what *your* feeling of Gratitude is. Close your eyes and think of something for which you are most easily thankful; a child, a house, a pet, a spouse, a recent raise in pay, whatever it may be. Feel what that Gratitude feels like in your body. Where do you feel it? What does it look like? Use all your senses to create a full, clear feeling picture. When done, open your eyes and make notes about the experience in your Oz Journal.

Also, practice being aware of when your energetic patterns are operating in your life; this in and of itself can be quite challenging. You are sure to go unconscious again and again even though you *know better*. That is all okay. Take it one day at a time: remember that you are not on some time schedule.

With practice you will be able to quickly determine when you have slipped back into unconsciousness. What does going unconscious look like? Going unconscious feels like you are operating on auto-pilot; just going through the movements or getting through the day. You will feel as if your energetic patterns are running the show and you have no say in the matter. You will be dragging yourself around, un-energized, unenthusiastic, numb, careless, and blah.

When you are conscious you feel that you have choices and that you are the master of your life. As the master of your life you can choose to be in Gratitude. With gratitude for you and everything within and around you, you feel awake and vibrant. So, all you have to do to bring yourself back to consciousness is to get back to Gratitude.

Be sure to write about your unconscious and conscious experiences in your Oz Journal. Make note of any conditions that you believe cause you to fall into an unconscious state; perhaps it is another person's energy or attitude, a smell, a food, a family situation.

Alternately, keep notes on conditions that help to keep you conscious; a certain time of day or place, a scent, a color, a memory, a feeling in your body. Whatever it is, write it down. By noting that which brings you to unconsciousness and that which keeps you conscious will go a long way in developing your ever expanding awareness.

Also, make special note of how it makes you *feel* when you do choose Gratitude.

It is absolutely fine if you experience feelings of frustration or annoyance; even when you choose the energetic pattern of Gratitude. Be thankful for these feelings as they are all clues that can aid you in your educational process.

Keep practicing Gratitude and magic will begin to unfold before you. The more you do so, the more you tip the scales in your favor and bring balance into your being.

Gratitude is your escape hatch from pain. Every time the unconsciously created energetic pattern comes up it is like receiving a call from your Soul saying, "Hey, this is still in here and creating pain, let's work on it now." And, if nothing else, you can at least be in Gratitude for this loving reminder.

Change your perspective from pain to Gratitude and you will change your energetic patterns; those created in density and darkness will change to patterns created from love and light.

2: Somewhere Over the Rainbow

Auntie Em suggests that Dorothy go to "where she won't get into any trouble." That sounds like a fine idea, but Dorothy wonders if a trouble-free place exists. She asks Toto if he supposes there is such a place, but Dorothy cannot hear his thoughts on the matter. None the less, she decides that there "must be" such a place, and that you can't get there "by a boat or a train."

Instead "It's far away. . ."

Oz Awareness #2: Our Limited View

As our dilemma/traumas and their resulting energetic patterns play out, we begin to believe in our limitations and view our lives from a very narrow perspective. We are conditioned to *know our limitations* and it is considered by our society to be *sensible* to know them and live by them. To think beyond society's sensible limitations is but a silly girl's dream. We believe and behave as if our dreams are beyond our limits, and live outside of us, existing Somewhere Over the Rainbow.

If we even dare to believe in a place where the skies are blue, dreams come true, and troubles melt like lemons drops, we are quite sure that we have not one clue on how to get there. But what we do have is a clue that this place exists.

It may exist in our dream world; it may be that place we go when we are lost in thought, or it may be what we call heaven. At the very least it is not a place that we believe we have the power to get to on our own accord. Instead, it is like an exclusive country club, meant only for those bluebirds born into the right family, or who are amazingly beautiful, or talented, or have an extremely high IQ. We do not have, nor do we know how to obtain, the Bluebird Club Membership Card.

Somewhere Over the Rainbow points to our *self-imposed* limitations and views. And we do not think we can move beyond these limitations for that would not be sensible.

Like Dorothy, we prove this to ourselves over and over again. When she ventures from the farm, *bad* things happen, Almira Gulch things happen. Try as she may, she cannot seem to escape the farm; it pulls her back each and every time. Even when later in the story she runs away, she is not gone very long before she finds herself running right back again.

But maybe, Dorothy is also being told that she need not ever leave the farm. That the rainbow she seeks is not as far away as she has deemed it to be.

Great and Powerful Perspective #2: Limitless Existence

Ideally, we would first see the beauty of this fine and perfect gift of limitation. For if we do not experience limitation, then how could we ever truly know, much less appreciate, our Limitless Existence?

When we experience our contracted existence and its resulting pain, we are being called to open ourselves up to the possibility of what *could be*. And when we open ourselves up to these possibilities, even more significant, when we open ourselves up to what we currently believe to be impossible, we begin to blur the lines of our self-imposed limitations and open ourselves up to making all things possible. We begin to experience our Limitless Existence.

We are provided with the opportunity to break through our limitations each and every time our dilemma/trauma arises, each time we say "I can't", and each time we see a small dull farm in a grayed out landscape and think "this is all there is?" These are each examples of opportunities to break out and open up to the idea that Somewhere Over the Rainbow truly does exist.

Somewhere Over the Rainbow tells us that we can transcend our limitations. We have a sense of this truth, but we tend to look in the wrong place, we look for the rainbow out there, missing the fact that the rainbow exists right where we stand. We need not go anywhere outside our little Kansas farm to find it, we can stay right in our own backyard and begin to experience Limitless Existence in the here and now.

One of the quickest ways to bring awareness to your Limitless Existence is to give yourself space to do so and to refrain from anything that is telling you otherwise. Seemingly innocuous activities are keeping you in a limited space and place. These activities have really got your attention and they are conditioning you, on a daily basis, to experience narrow existence and further build your own walls of self-imposed limitations.

To begin with, consider your news and media habit. Do these things really enhance your life? They are filled with negativity, opinions, and judgments. They tell you how to act, feel, and look. They tell you what is important and what you need right now in order to be oh-so-happy. Does this promote authenticity? Does this promote a Soul focused life? At the very least, begin to question these sources and wonder at their truth for *you*.

Begin to also question any person, institution, or organization that is telling you how to behave, believe, think or be. Though they may not necessarily have mal-intent, they may not be speaking on behalf of *your* Soul. You are a unique aspect of All That Is, allow that uniqueness to begin to shine through and guide you. Write about any of your thoughts in your Oz Journal.

Once you have opened up this space and therefore opened up your awareness to your self-imposed limitations, you can begin to bring a meditative awareness to everything you do. Meditation is something that we do each day. It comes to us very naturally.

We tend to view our moments of meditation as "spacing out" or wonder "where we went" as we pull into our driveway with no direct recollection of how we got there. Realize that you were simply falling into a natural meditation.

Consciously setting aside time to sit in meditation is highly recommended. I do it every day, as do several other people on this Earth. When I first started meditating I was positive I was doing it wrong; I could not sit still without my grocery list popping into my head, or past occurrences playing over in my mind. But over time, as I continued to *practice*, it became something that I just do. I now fall into meditation easily.

If you feel called to learn to meditate, I highly recommend you do so. All it requires is a little bit of time and commitment. Do not force it, just sit and be quiet and keep sitting and being quiet and one day, you will have an awareness that you are meditating.

When thoughts pop up just let them go. If it is something you want to remember, see yourself placing it in a treasure chest or handing it over to your angels and know that it will come back to you later.

You may want to start with a guided meditation recording, and then go it on your own when you feel comfortable. You are looking for silent awareness, but at the same time please realize that meditation is not goal-oriented. There is not one place to get to, and that when you get there you are done. Just as in any, for example, athletic pursuit you can always go further, and each goal simply opens the door to another.

It can take some time to get to a point where you feel you are actually meditating. Remember that there is no time schedule. No one is counting the days for you to become an enlightened meditation master. You are the only one that can impose time limitations on your self, so just *do not do it*. Free yourself of this need.

You can also begin to practice a meditative life by bringing a meditative focus to a few things you do each day. For example, commit to a meditative focus when you cook dinner and when you brush your teeth. Then, before bed, you could perhaps light a candle and meditate on the flame for just five minutes.

While you cook dinner, brush your teeth or softly gaze into the candle flame, focus on that activity only. Do not listen to the news, do not obsess about what a relative did or said, do not plan the next picnic outing; simply focus on the activity at hand. Clear mind while cooking, clear mind while brushing teeth, clear mind while flame gazing. Feel free to write about any impressions and experiences in your Oz Journal.

As these activities become easier, choose more activities for meditative focus. The more you focus on what you are doing at any given moment, the more you allow your life to become Soul focused. Having this sort of focus takes far less energy and creates easy flow. It is in meditation that we meet our Soul. Plan to meet with it more often!

3: Almira Gulch

Dorothy, fresh from lemon drop dreams in a trouble-free zone, is just about to meet a real sour puss face to face, and this is Almira Gulch.

When Ms. Gulch makes a visit to the farm to confront Uncle Henry and Auntie Em, she is steamed.   Toto has had one too many romps in her flower beds and one too many run-ins with her cat. We also learn that Toto has apparently bitten her on the leg. That leg bite was the last straw and now Almira comes armed with a sheriff's order to take Toto away.

She literally wants to have Toto "destroyed", which sure seems a bit harsh. Toto is but a wee little dog, not some vicious junkyard behemoth. None the less, Almira's got it out for Toto and if the Gale residence does not see fit to cooperate, she threatens a "damage suit that'll take your farm."

Almira Gulch is not fooling around; she owns a good portion of the county, and feels that this ownership gives her the right to wield power and make over the top threats. Dorothy calls it like it is, calling her a "wicked old witch."

Whatever the case, Almira has her sheriff's order, allowing her to remove Toto. And since Uncle Henry and Auntie Em are upstanding, law-abiding citizens, they stand aside, allowing her to take Toto away.

Dorothy now finds herself without her beloved companion, Toto, while Uncle Henry and Auntie Em have been threatened with the loss of their farm.

Oz Awareness #3: Our Viral Dilemmas

We can only speculate as to how Dorothy's original dilemma/trauma could span out from here. We can guess that if Uncle Henry and Auntie Em were to lose the farm it would certainly affect the entire Gale residence, along with the farmhands and their families. Like a virus the dilemma/trauma will span out to the county at large and so on and so on.

We see in this scene how the original dilemma/trauma can become completely lost to us. As it makes its way through our life and the lives of others, layers and layers of dilemma/traumas result, one stacking on top of the other. What began as a puppy romp through the flower beds, is now threatening livelihoods.

As we talked about before, the dilemma/trauma has led to an energetic pattern that will not simply disappear. If left unchecked the energetic pattern will continue to become bigger and more apparent, affecting more and more beings, and leading to even more noticeable imbalances.

Our imbalances can show up in our physical body as a disease, for example. It can also show up as a mental disorder, angry outburst, poverty, addiction, or dysfunction in any area of life. Whatever the case, it is not something that affects you and only you.

Eventually, it affects your family, then spans out from there; to your pet friends, the energy in your house, the water your drink, all can be affected by this energy imbalance.

Everything is connected to everything; therefore an imbalance in one creates an imbalance in all. This is difficult for us to see in our dense, third dimensional world. We may be able to see it on a smaller scale. For example, how an imbalance in a particular eco-system is affecting the plant life in that area, or how an alcoholic father is affecting his family and co-workers. But these are tiny little hints as to the greater ripple effect; what you do will continue to spread out and affect everything. We are not perceptive enough to know how we affect All That Is, but we do.

As we looked at before, we can choose a new energetic pattern of gratitude that is based in love and light. This will then begin to override the energetic patterns created unconsciously in density. There is yet another energetic pattern that can bring great freedom to us. And this is the energetic pattern of Forgiveness.

Great and Powerful Perspective #3: Forgiveness is Freedom

We have been conditioned to the denser views of Forgiveness. We believe that there are things that are absolutely unforgivable. Also, we may think that when we forgive we are somehow condoning the behavior or giving permission for the behavior to continue. Sometimes when we forgive, we may do so in an ego-ic way, feeling as if we are the better person and have sunk down to another's lowly level and forgiven them from our pedestal of all that is righteous and good.

From the perspective of our Soul, Forgiveness is freedom. When we forgive we free ourselves and others from the energetic ties that keep us dwelling in dilemma/trauma darkness.
Forgiveness from the Soul says "I forgive you, and in this forgiveness I free myself from pain and

allow myself to heal and live in a more expansive way."

We can forgive anyone at any time and anywhere. We do not have to call them on the phone or write them a letter, we just forgive them. Be they now living on this Earth or even if they have since passed, we can forgive them; for Forgiveness knows no boundaries.

It can be as easy as saying, "I (your name) forgive (person's name) fully and completely." Or perhaps you would like to write it down. There is a practice that suggests doing as Jesus says to do, and that is to forgive seventy times seven times. Each day, for seven days in a row (no skipping days) you write the aforementioned statement down seventy times. You can forgive anyone, including yourself, as well as anything; like food, religion, sex, etc.

We could take this a step further by simply forgiving ourselves *only*. When we forgive ourselves, we free ourselves. In this case say, or write down, "I (your name) forgive myself for (being angry with, feeling betrayed by, being jealous of, etc.) (person's name)." You may think that I am being quite cheeky for even suggesting this. If you were wronged, why should you even bother forgiving *yourself* for what another has done to you?

The short answer is, to free you from the energetic ties that hold you in a stuck pattern. The longer answer is that, on a level currently hidden from you, you called in the situation that is now calling for Forgiveness. You called it in energetically, and more than likely, unconsciously. Perhaps you called it in to heal something from your past, perhaps you called it in to create maturity and growth; there could be many reasons. And now it is being played out on your life stage and you now have a choice. You can wallow in it or you can learn and therefore heal from it.

Whatever the case, the energy of true Forgiveness works for you in your favor and in the favor of those around you, and it will continue to span out.

You will know when you have truly forgiven, as you will no longer harbor low vibrational feelings, what we may call negative feelings, for the person or feel that they owe you something. You will be able to think about yourself and the person without dark emotions welling up inside.

This works both ways, if you have done something for which you wish to be forgiven, please do apologize to whomever you need to. If they will not forgive you or even see you or talk to you, then know that you can forgive yourself on your own accord. By changing the energetic pattern to one of Forgiveness you can change the relationship, even if the person is not right there in front of you or willing to participate.

I offer past life regression to client's that come to me for healing. One client came to me and was upset about the relationship she had with her sister, they had not talked for over two years. During the session she was shown three past lives; each of these lives had been shared with her now current sister.

The day after the session, my client contacted me and was ecstatic as her sister had just called her, seemingly out of the blue. During the session, something was released and healed, leaving her and her sister with the opportunity to reconnect and begin anew.

I realize that you may not believe in past lives and may be put off by this. Please hang in with me here. It does not matter if you believe it to be true or not; what matters is that for this particular individual this therapy worked to bring a healing to her and her sister. It opened a door that gave her and her sister an opportunity to heal.

At the very least, be willing to consider that what we have come to *know* on Earth, from this most dense existence, does not provide us with the fuller picture that can be viewed from the higher vantage point of our Soul.

On your own you can repeat the Forgiveness exercises as often as necessary. Write down your exercises as well as your experiences of Forgiveness in your Oz Journal.

You can stop the viral affects of your dilemma/traumas within yourself and your outer world. Do not get caught up in who wronged who, and when and why. Bring freedom to you and others through Forgiveness.

4. Dorothy Runs Away

Almira Gulch, now thinking she has everything under control, has put Toto in a basket and is determinedly biking back from whence she came, or perhaps to go wreak havoc on some other county resident's life. It does not take long for Toto to peek his little head out of the basket, hop out and run back to Dorothy.

Dorothy is, of course, thrilled to see Toto, but she knows that someone will be back to retrieve him and she is not about to stick around to find out. So she packs up a suitcase and her own basket and runs away.

Oz Awareness #4: Our Fearful Reactions

We have all been here. When our dilemma/traumas do not magically disappear on their own, we react by running. We may run away from our dilemma/trauma literally by skipping town, or we run away figuratively through avoidance and disregard. What we find is that neither of these reactions work; no matter how far or how fast we run, dilemma/traumas have a way of catching up with us.

Rather than run, we are being called to face our dilemma/traumas. By facing and releasing, we open up to our true power. And when we stand in our true power we lead with our Soul. We stop reacting to outside circumstances by running away and we begin to calmly turn our attention inward.

Faux power, like that demonstrated by Almira Gulch (and later as the Wicked Witch of the West) is power that is wielded outside; it is the supposed power that comes with money, status, weaponry, dogma, political hierchy and the like. This sort of power is ego-ic in nature. When we wield power with our bank accounts, guns, and ownership of things or knowledge, we become bullies. We begin to measure our *power* by the amount of fear we can instill in others.

Faux power can be quite clever. For example, there are *powers* that claim to have our best interest at hand and prove this by consistently showing us examples of how they are keeping us safe. At the same time, it is these very same powers that are preaching fear to us at every turn. They tell us that their laws, programs, products, institutions and dogma were created to keep us safe; but it is their very laws, programs, products, institutions and dogma that keep us in a state of fear. We are told over and over again to follow the plans that they have outlined for us or else something horrible and detrimental will assuredly come to pass.

True power comes from a place where bulk, brawn and bombs are not needed. True power is rooted in love. True power comes to us as we raise our vibrational level and gain the ability to stop non-loving actions and thoughts simply by being present and by being of love and light.

As we continually choose to allow things that are outside of our selves to convince us that we are not powerful, we hide from our Soul; all but forgetting of its existence.

We are like Dorothy in that we do not believe in our true power. We believe in a power that comes from that which others have and in which we are lacking; like money, status, and fame. Yet, we have seen it over and over again; these things do not bring true power. We have seen CEOs, celebrities and the like all fall from *power*. And why is this? It is because their power did not come from within.

Great and Powerful Perspective #4: True Power through Our Inner Voice

Now is the time to stand in our True Power. We can do this when we stop running and start listening. We each have a powerful Inner Voice and this voice speaks from the level of our Soul.

We tend to diminish the importance of our Inner Voice, treating it as if it is a preposterous puppy notion. We get a nudge, a tap, or an inkling, and rather than listen to it, we run away from it and choose a fearful reaction.

If we were to sit down and list the things we do based on fear, be it fear we have actually experienced personally or fear based on what has happened to another, we would be mighty surprised. We do everything from buying certain brands of clothes and cars, to choosing spouses and life insurance policies, from a stance of fear.

On the other hand, when we commit to the wisdom of our Inner Voice, we align with our Soul and we end up in a much more enlightened place. We can pretend like we cannot speak the language of our Inner Voice; we can make it out to be a nuisance and we can believe that we cannot hear it. We can suppose that there are but a few who have *the gift* or ability to hear their Inner Voice. We can do all these things, but that does not change the fact that each of us has one.

And our Inner Voice is with us, in every dilemma/trauma, as well as in every happy moment. No matter how far we run it is always there, always talking to us, always waiting for us to tune in.

Everyone has been gifted with an Inner Voice. And as we head into our next evolution, the veil that has kept us from easy access to our Inner Voice is lifting.

Realize that when you fall back on excuses like, "I am just not really intuitive", or "I've tried to hear my inner voice, but it is not very talkative", you are choosing to close yourself off to that which is your birth right. It was given to you as a way to stay in touch with your divinity, your guides, your angels, and your Eternal Family; beings that have known you since your very very beginnings. It was given to you as a way to know your connection with God and All That Is.

As children, we are highly intuitive. Then as we grow older and become ensconced into the collective consciousness of our clan – family, community, religion, school, or vocation – we became indoctrinated into denser belief systems that began to blind us from our greater being. Reclaim your broader sight now; get in touch with your Inner Voice, get in touch with your Toto; for it is Toto that represents the Inner Voice in our story.

So far in our story, we might assume that trouble and Toto go hand in hand. Instead, however, Toto is talking to Dorothy and attempting to lead her in a more healing direction. What Toto has been trying to convey to Dorothy is the very same thing that our own Inner Voices are trying to convey to us. Toto wants Dorothy to face her Almira Gulch dilemma/traumas and open up to the guidance of the Inner Voice. If we could open up to our own Inner Voices we would no longer need to run, we could stop running, become calm and listen.

The best way to open up to your Inner Voice is to practice. In your Oz Journal, begin keeping simple notations of how you use your intuition for guidance, as well as ways in which you go against its guidance By writing these examples down, you will become more attentive as to what your Inner Voice *sounds* like and how you can be more aware of it and further open up to it.

Small things really do count, so be sure to always make a note of them. And do not get caught up in needing *proof.* For example, one day I was getting my daughter ready for school, and I felt as if I should keep her with me for the day. There was no sensible reason for this. When I *checked in* with my Inner Voice, I began to tear up and for me this is always an indication that what I am feeling is very real and in line with what my Inner Voice is telling me. So I didn't send her to school.

Thankfully, nothing out of sorts happened at the school that day, and I may never know why I was meant to keep her at home, but I honored my Inner Voice and did just that.

Your Inner Voice is dynamite at making your everyday life flow in a subtle yet easier manner. I use it daily. Sometimes I find myself making a purchase for something I do not need, but my Inner Voice tells me that I should just go ahead and buy it. Later on that day or week I understand why I needed to buy it and am thankful that I am not running out at the last minute to purchase it.

Other times, I end up not purchasing something because my Inner Voice is saying, "no need to buy this." I then end up acquiring it through other means. By listening to our Inner Voice we save time, money, frustration and hassle.

You can practice using your intuition the next time you go out and do a little shopping and by noticing your feelings while purchasing or not purchasing certain items. Another way to practice is to guess who is calling on you when the phone rings or when there is a knock at the door or when you hear an email pop into your in-box. Look for other opportunities to practice using your Inner Voice and as you rely on it more and more, you will find that your life becomes ever more graceful and easy.

Yes, it may be difficult at first. You are learning a whole new way of being. So do be gentle with yourself, be kind to yourself during this learning process and love yourself for improving your state of being with each passing moment. Do not get upset when you believe you have misheard. First of all, I cannot tell you how many times my *mis-hears* have proved themselves to be right-ons down the line. Also, just as when you are learning anything that is new to you, you learn just as much from the mistakes. Keep this in mind.

Listening to your Inner Voice brings ease and flow to you. Learn to listen and behold wonder!

5. Crystal Gazing

When Dorothy runs away she soon finds herself in the presence of Professor Marvel. Professor Marvel claims to be *Acclaimed by the Crowned Heads of Europe* and is a man of many talents; he can read "your past, present and future in his crystal," he is a juggler, a sleight of hand artist and a balloon exhibitionist.

Of course we quickly gather that Professor Marvel is a bit over reaching in his claims. While talking to Dorothy, he slips up and reveals that he does not really know any crowned heads of Europe. Also, in order for him to gather any information by gazing into his crystal, he must first distract Dorothy and gaze into the contents of her wicker basket. His *revelations* are merely common sense assumptions and we find ourselves marveling at his cheeky ways.

In his crystal ball he *sees* Auntie Em falling ill with a broken heart, causing Dorothy to become visibly upset. She then gathers up all her things and hurries back to the farm. Even though the wind is pitching a fit and some rather violent weather is about to let loose, Professor Marvel, this seer of the future, allows Dorothy, a mere little girl, to just take off.

Oz Awareness #5: Distraction and Illusion

Professor Marvel represents Distraction and Illusion. And it is on Earth that we fully engage in Distraction and Illusion. So much so that we are oblivious to the fact that what we see around us and right in front of us is just that; Distraction and Illusion.

We are gazing at Distraction and Illusion all the time, they are right there in front of us, always and everywhere, but we are completely unaware that they are diverting our attention or hiding our Soul from us.

Of course, there are the obvious distractions and illusions; addictions to drugs, cigarettes, video games, television, shopping and food. But there is a less obvious and seemingly innocent addiction that is pervasive in our society, and this is the addiction to our *comfortable* boxes.

We build up these boxes on our own and choose to live in them, all but refusing to emerge from them. What we fail to realize is that these boxes do not have to contain us on a permanent basis. We always have the choice to move out. These boxes are just another form of running away. We *run away* from what we most need to pay attention to by distracting ourselves and actively participating in illusion.

Perhaps we live in a *comfortable* box of abuse. We know this box because we spent our childhood in a similar one. As an adult we chose, unconsciously, to make a lateral move into another abusive box. And we stay there; same box, different address. And we think we cannot leave because we are fearful of the unknown, for at the very least we understand and have learned the language of the abusive box. And there is a certain comfort in that; even though it is actually quite uncomfortable

Our abusive boxes can all look very different. In one, the abuse is to one's own being through the use of harmful substances. In another, the abuse is experienced at the hand of another who abuses us physically, mentally, sexually and/or emotionally. In yet another, the abuse may be through the abuse of our trust. Whatever the case, we live in this box and have spent so much time and energy building it that we cannot see a way out.

We can also look at how we constantly allow other *boxes* to create Distraction and Illusion in which we all participate. We get in our car and turn on the radio *box*; we come home and turn on the TV *box*. And through all of these boxes we are informed about other boxes. We place a lot of importance on these boxes; buying even bigger and more powerful ones. We buy the boxes that the other boxes are telling us about; boxes of food, boxes with information guaranteed to make us smarter, boxes that come with free boxes and boxes that will transform us from "before" to "after." We then spend time researching boxes, working to have money to buy the boxes, and then comparing our boxes with everyone else's boxes.

So how do we begin to break out of our box fixations and see the greater reality? How do we begin to see the reality that nourishes our Soul, as opposed to depleting our being?

It begins with putting our Awareness on it. And the more we put our Awareness on it, the more we discover and the more we reveal. As we reveal ourselves to our Souls, we become more comfortable with change. As we become comfortable with change we gain resilience and adaptability, placing us in closer alignment with All That Is.

Great and Powerful Perspective #5: Awareness

We have already talked about Awareness in this book, but now we put it front and center. Without Awareness we will consistently miss out on opportunities for growth and maturity.

Obviously, if you are addicted to a harmful substance, like cigarettes or alcohol, for example, these are addictions that keep you from purity in body and that cause you to use your energy and time for things that do not bring nourishment and joy.

These types of addictions can seem beyond difficult to release and overcome. There is a great entanglement of fear in addiction, and an even greater fear in quitting the addiction. We have all been told again and again how practically impossible it can be to quit, as countless have returned to their addictions over and over again.

But perhaps this is due to the fact that most of the attention is put on the actual quitting or avoidance of the addictive substance, both of which can deplete our energy. If we were to put our Awareness on our true power and purpose, then we would be placing attention on that which can nourish us.

The same applies to our comfortable boxes. We put most of our attention on how to escape outwardly, as opposed to becoming intimate with our inner true power and purpose. If you or anyone else is in danger, then you must escape from the comfortable box without delay. But in order to not return to that box, you must immediately take to going inward and begin to touch the power that lies within; again and again until it becomes evident in your everyday existence.

Spend some time writing about how your addictions keep you distracted from standing in your true power and living your true purpose. What could you do if you did not have the

addiction? How would you spend your time?
What would your life look like? Make a list of what
you could and would do. Write them down in
small, easy to manage baby steps, and then begin
to do them one by one, day by day.

Also write down what you need to focus on outside
of the addiction *and* inside of you. Do *not* focus on
what you do *not* want! You are not going to focus
on not smoking or not drinking alcohol.

When the US started the War on Drugs, drugs
became more abundant, more addictive and more
dangerous. We focused on what we did not want;
we did not want drugs. Instead of the War on
Drugs, perhaps we would have made greater
gains by focusing on what we do want. Perhaps
the campaign should have been called Peace in
Life.

Focus on what you *do* want. If you want to be a
writer, begin by writing a paragraph about
something that touched you, write about the
amazing array of unique snowflakes that fall

abundantly on a winter's eve or write love notes to your Soul. If you want to be healthy, start eating one piece of fruit a day, do five minutes of movement, buy an unusual vegetable and learn how to cook it.

If you live in an abusive household and need to get out, seek out appropriate professionals that make it their business to help abused persons; perhaps call a law official or a shelter. This is not the time to be embarrassed, this is the time to stand up for yourself and live your life the way you want.

All of this will go a long way in releasing an addiction. Also, consider visiting an energy healer of high intention. These healers can be invaluable. Energy healers deal at the energetic level and support you in moving out dark energy and moving in love and light. There are numerous forms of energy healing; Reiki, Rebirthing, sound healing, chakra balancing, past life regression, acupuncture, Qi Gong, Tai Chi, Kundalini Yoga; the list goes on and on.

I have personally dealt with some heavy addictions and have come out of them a wiser, more enlightened person. As strange as it may sound, I would not have traded any of it; the maturity and growth I have experienced as a result of the gift of the addictions is fascinating and worthy of honor.

I too was once under the illusion that I was powerless, but as I released addiction, I began to stand more in my true power and live in my true purpose. You can too. I have nothing more or less than do you. At the energetic level we truly are equal.

Distraction and Illusion is layered. As your awareness expands you will come upon new insights. Simply by turning your awareness to you, you engage what is known as the "observer effect"; meaning that your mere observance can and does have an effect on what is being observed. Be sure to keep notes about this in your Oz Journal. Write them all down, no matter how insignificant you may think they are.

As you practice your awareness you will eventually begin to find less obvious distractions. These distractions may seem harmless, but they too are keeping you from being in alignment and on purpose.

For example, one day I was off to run errands. I planned on running by the library, and since I would be in town I thought I may stop into a few stores to see if I could find any good deals and pick up a few items from our always present grocery list. I dropped the kids off to school and was about to go on my way when I got thinking about the day. I realized that I was about to distract myself from making my day count for something.

The librarians were not holding their breath awaiting my arrival, I had no need to truly find any deals on anything and the grocery list could wait for well over a week. I was simply distracting myself from being in alignment and on purpose; which just happened to be the writing of this book.

I drove back to my house. I spent some time in silence and meditation, and then sat down to my computer to write. By the time I was off to pick up my children at the end of the school day, I was re-energized about my writing and could not wait to get back to it. I made my day count.

So do spend some time placing your awareness on all that you do. What do you spend time doing? Are these activities taking you away from aligning with your true purpose? What is your true purpose today and what will it be in the future? Everyday, check in and see how you can make your day count.

Stop hiding behind your own Distraction and Illusion. Bring awareness to all areas of your life. Disconnect from the media, especially the television, the radio and any internet sites that cater to news/gossip/etc. As you disconnect from these, intend to connect to that higher aspect of you; your Soul. As you do so your inner voice will become clearer. Your awareness will become unbounded.

And trust that you will become even more informed, as the information is coming from a much higher place. And know that you will not miss out on anything.

I love meteor showers and one night I awoke from sleep with the notion that I should get up and look out my bedroom window. I saw a shooting star, then another, then another, then another. I lay down on the floor and watched this amazing display for about an hour. I did not need to find out about the meteor shower from TV or any other source outside of myself; instead, my Soul let me know.

Disengage from Distraction and Illusion; it creates pain and confusion. Bring in awareness and re-engage your Soul.

6. Its a Twister

Dorothy takes off for the farm to face the latest dilemma/trauma, a broken hearted Auntie Em. Meanwhile, Auntie Em is looking for Dorothy, but is unable to find her. A tornado looms in the not so far off distance and the farm folk must head into the cellar.

By the time Dorothy returns, the twister is practically on top of her. She runs through the house, to the cellar and back through the house again; literally running in circles as if she is embodying the twister. The twister has her in its path and she is fully engaging in its chaos.

Oz Awareness #6: Blaming Solves Nothing

The twister is symbolic of a dilemma/trauma, and its resulting energetic pattern, spinning out of control. Each of us has our own unique twister(s); DWI, job loss, nervous breakdown, disease.

Whatever your twister is, it is noticeable and can no longer be disregarded.

The twister is obvious. It is a huge wake up call to heal ourselves.

And just as in every situation, we are at choice. We can sit down, give up, wallow and let the twister have its way with us, or we can choose to move into its calm center and be with it; it is here that we can most effectively and efficiently heal.

Our tendency is to blame others for the twister. When we blame someone else, we think that we are *freeing* ourselves from the responsibility of having to do anything about it. We choose to wait around for the other person to fix it, or tell us that they are sorry for what they have done, or provide us with something that will allow us to move on. While we wait around for this to come to pass, we find ourselves spinning in circles. We are like a broken record, saying over and over again, "I am not going to do anything about it because it is not *my* fault."

We remain tethered to the energies that keep us in a cyclone of pain and trauma. We give up our power and remain stuck in the energy. We find our mind running around in circles, playing situations over and over again in our heads, coming up with witty "should-have-saids" and scheming on how we will behave when the other person finally sees fit to do something about it. And we wait. And we wait.

We are just like Dorothy, spinning about, and feeling out of control and powerless; giving into to the twister-chaos.

Great and Powerful Perspective #6: Personal Responsibility

Just as we learned from Chapter 3, we can free ourselves with forgiveness. We can also free ourselves when we take Personal Responsibility for our lives. When we blame others we end up energetically tied to the twister and allow another to hold the reigns while we wallow in self-pity and victimhood.

We can free ourselves right where we stand and not wait another moment by taking Personal Responsibility for everything in our lives. Even that in which we do not seem to share any bit of fault; even that which seems to have been dumped in our laps.

I am going to share with you a personal example from my own life. This story is about my adopted son, whom my husband and I adopted when he was four years of age. For he is by far the most obvious twister tearing through my life.

To put it mildly, my son had a rather rocky start. He was traumatized and abused on many levels by his birth mother and birth grandparents. Though we were loving parents, he did not seem to want our love, no matter what we said or did.

He seemed impenetrable to love. And when one does not allow love in, one cannot grow and expand and one becomes evermore contracted. As a result, my son was unable to mature and grow. On top of it, as the years rolled along, he began to display disturbing behaviors. The older he got the disturbing behaviors became dangerous.

After years of therapies and therapists, we finally came to learn that he had something called Reactive Attachment Disorder (RAD). RAD is an inability to attach with the caregiver. Children with RAD lack trust completely. They are in a perpetual state of survival mode. They have no conscience and a high level of shame, are outrageously narcissistic, super self-centered and the ultimate control freaks. They can be quite charming to outsiders, but are absolute monsters to those closest to them.

People with RAD are far more removed from their divinity than most; they barely even know they are human. They vibrate extremely low and are the densest amongst us. If you think of the infamous who have created the greatest atrocities known to us, you know what a RAD person is capable of. At their most extreme RAD people are sociopaths; they fill our jails and exist at the center of many an abusive home.

For years I was beyond angry with his birth mother, the Department of Family Services and his foster family. I was incensed that no one had even hinted to the hell that lie before us. I was infuriated that though I did not create this mess, I was going to have to be the one to clean it up.

I could write an entire book about the horrors that have gone on and continue to go on in my house. Out of respect for my son, I will not do so in these pages. Perhaps this is something I will take on at another time, for I do feel called to help my fellow adoptive families. Many of us suffer in shame and silence at the hands of our severely traumatized children.

For now, I will share with you that as a healer, and a parent for that matter, I have learned that in the end, the ultimate healing is up to the *healee*. My son is either going to accept love, and therefore healing, or not; I cannot say. Regardless of what the people in our lives decide to choose, we are called to choose Personal Responsibility for our own lives.

My husband and I worked very closely with a RAD therapist in order to heal our son. She taught us various ways to parent this type of child, which is not the parenting you read about in books or share with friends. It is a rather overwhelming task. We have altered practically every area of our lives, many times over, to make space for healing to happen.

During this same time, my husband and I chose to take Personal Responsibility for our own lives; we realized that we had to begin to work on our own childhood dilemma/traumas. We realized that part of the purpose of parenting our son was to accept this opportunity for our own healing.

Personally, I needed to release the pattern of abuse that had existed with me since being sexually molested by a neighbor as a child. I realized that the same feelings I experienced at the time of the sexual abuse, were all being played out before me again. I felt scared, ashamed, betrayed, and imprisoned.

My son scared me. I was ashamed at my naiveté and that I had allowed him into my life. I felt betrayed by the system and had become a prisoner in my own house. His constant abuse was distressing and damaging. I had moved from one abusive box and into another. These realizations were astonishing and lead to my own healing in numerous areas and levels of my life.

As my husband and I began to heal, we changed. We both began to stand in our true power, more and more each day. And as our son continues to lash out, we become even more powerful. It is our responsibility to continue to grow in strength for him, as well as for our daughter.

We have worked diligently and lovingly with our son for over ten years, perhaps one day all that time and energy will be evident in the person we know he can be. It is our greatest and most profound wish that one day, our son take Personal Responsibility for his darkness and step into the light that awaits him at every turn.

When we take Personal Responsibility we do so with great commitment and courage. We are able to step into the calm center of the twister and heal at the very core. As we do so, we become more aware and begin to discover the whole of ourselves; physically, mentally, emotionally and spiritually.

So do yourself a huge favor and stop waiting for someone else to heal you. Ask yourself who, or even what, you are allowing to block the path to your healing. Who do you blame for what became of you? How does blaming them hinder your life? Does it keep you stuck or keep you chasing that which always seems to elude you? Write about this in your Oz Journal.

When you commit to healing yourself and take Personal Responsibility for everything in your life, you change yourself at an energetic level. No longer do you align with low vibrations, instead you invite in higher and higher vibrations, each time coming closer and closer to joy.

7. Inside the Cyclone

In Dorothy's last run through the house, she is struck in the head by a loosed window and falls unconscious onto the bed. When Dorothy comes to, the house is spinning wildly about. She stands up to look outside the window and sees all sorts of crazy things flying along with her; chickens, a cow, and fishermen in a boat. One of the *visitors* at Dorothy's window is Almira Gulch, who, while riding the wind on her bike, turns into a broom-wielding witch.

The house finally lands with a thump, and Dorothy gets up and walks warily to the front door. As she opens the door, she emerges from the gray washed Kansas landscape and is delivered into a vibrant new world filled with color and beauty. In this new world, the water is bluer than blue, the flowers are larger than large; everything is blooming and bright and beckoning.

She says, "Toto, I have a feeling we're not in Kansas anymore." Then with excited realization she proclaims, "We must be over the rainbow!"

An orb then floats down from the sky, turning into Glinda the Good Witch of the North. Glinda shares two important bits of information with Dorothy. First, that her house has landed, and subsequently destroyed, the Wicked Witch of the East. Second, she is in a place called Munchkin Land, and that due to her *lucky* aim, she has been proclaimed as the Munchkins' national heroine.

Oz Awareness #7: Our Soul Mind Knows All

The seemingly unrelated items that Dorothy sees outside the window of the spinning house are not to be discounted as mere Hollywood folly. They represent the symbols, images and pictures of our subconscious mind, or Soul Mind.

When we sleep, meditate, or are in a state of hypnosis, we are accessing our Soul Mind. The language of the Soul Mind is that of symbols, images and pictures. In fact, we can unlock many of our own mysteries by having an intimate connection with this world; by placing awareness and making note of these symbols we are creating yet another vehicle by which we can open up to our authenticity and true power.

When Dorothy sees Almira Gulch turn into the Wicked Witch she is provided with a hint that not all is as it seems. It would seem that the tornado storm is heralding in the great big winds of change.

The destruction of the Wicked Witch of the East is representative of the release of an energetic pattern. And when we release one pattern, we invite ourselves to additional release.

Do not miss the brilliance of this scene. When Dorothy lands in Munchkin Land, Dorothy lands right smack dab in the middle of her childhood dilemma/traumas. The Munchkins, who are little adult people with childish mannerisms, represent us as adults trapped in our own childhood dilemma/traumas.

If we were to look at ourselves in a truthful way, we may recognize times in our adult life when we behave in childlike ways. These behaviors point to trauma experienced in childhood. We become stuck in the energy of that trauma and its resulting energetic pattern. This then becomes the consciousness from which we operate. And each time we choose these childish behaviors, we deny ourselves an opportunity for maturity and growth.

On the whole, Oz represents our Soul Mind; all of our experiences, existences, and memories are stored in this hidden part of us. It is hidden only because we have allowed it to be so; now is the time to wake up to it. Most of us are afraid to *go there*, we are afraid of what we may find. We are afraid of what we will face, we are afraid to call upon all those dilemma/traumas and say, "Come out, come out, wherever you are."

When we open ourselves up to our Soul Mind we invite release, healing and change. We go into that infinite, all-knowing part of ourselves. We begin to step out from our grayed out existence and choose colorful beautiful brightness.

Great and Powerful Perspective #7: Embrace Your Infinite Soul

On Earth we are bound by time and space and this boundary is not a punishment. Rather, it provides us with a unique opportunity for amazing and explosive expansion. It may sound strange; we are *bound* by time and space and this will in turn create *expansion*?

Yes. Because, by completely forgetting whom we really are, which we have done quite successfully, we have allowed ourselves to experience density in its fullness. With density comes separative-ness; a feeling that we are not connected, we are individual, we are country, flag, borders, us and them. With density comes pain and fear; feeling that we are not safe, feeling that we must lash out on self and others in order to protect us from them. And with density come the distractions and illusions that keep us believing we are powerless, wallowing victims.

Now, we are invited to emerge from that density. (Welcome to the next phase of the human evolution, be the first on your block and begin emerging today!) We are invited to feel and know the Oneness, to know our power and settle into the ever present safety of God's arms.

And because we are coming to this feeling and knowing it from a place of density, we are allowing for ever more expansive growth, because we are now going to experience our Infinite Soul, while at the same time being in physical form. It's the best of both worlds!

Right now we are RAD children. We do not trust our caregiver; we are not allowing in the fullness of love, we are in an ego filled existence of survival mode. Our primary caregiver, God, has all the love we will ever need; if we could just put complete trust in and surrender to God and Soul. We are now being offered the opportunity to just be and stop exhausting ourselves with doing, doing and more doing.

Our Soul exists outside of time and space; therefore it has always been and will always be. It is Infinite. Know this. Be aware of your Soul in this way. When you think about you, think about yourself in this expansive way. You are a master. You are now experiencing a re-awakening to that mastery.

Look back in time and wonder at how long you, as Soul, have been here. Look forward in time and wonder at how much further you have to be. It is Infinite. You have all the time in the Universe. This is *awe*-some, and so much fun to be in and play with. Open up to this knowledge and muse on how it can completely alter the life you are currently living.

What if you could stop doing all you do to stay safe and just be in each blissful moment? What would your life look like? What if you could feel and know your Infinite Soul? Write about this in your Oz Journal.

8. Dorothy Meets the Wicked Witch of the West

The Munchkins celebrate the death of the Wicked Witch of the East with dance, song, declarations and gifts to Dorothy. But their celebration comes to an abrupt end when they receive a surprise visit from the Wicked Witch of the West, who also happens to be the sister to the now dead Wicked Witch of the East. She has come to find out who killed her sister.

Dorothy is quick to point out that it was an accident and was completely unintentional. The Witch, however, is not going to accept some wimpy apology. She threatens Dorothy, telling her that she can "cause accidents, too." Glinda diverts the Witch's attention by reminding her about the Ruby Slippers on her sister's feet. And just as she leans down to retrieve them, they disappear, only to re-appear on Dorothy's feet where, as Glinda says, "There they are and there they'll stay."

Dorothy looks down in disbelief, she has no idea how they got on her feet and she does not look too sure about keeping them. The Witch demands that Dorothy give the Ruby Slippers back to her as she is "the only one that knows how to use them." But Glinda whispers to Dorothy to "Keep tight inside of them" as their magic is apparently quite powerful or why else would the Witch pine for them so.

The Witch tells Glinda to butt out and threatens Glinda, but Glinda just laughs, reminding the Witch that she has "no power here." The Witch decides that she will therefore bide her time, but she doesn't leave without threatening Dorothy, "I'll get you, my pretty, and your little dog, too." And off she goes in a sulfur puff of smoke and fire.

Oz Awareness #8: Our Powerful Foundation

In this scene we are given a preview of the power struggle about to ensue. It is the Self versus the ego. In our story, the ego is played by Almira Gulch and her *alter ego* the Wicked Witch of the West. We see that she has pretty much been running the show when it comes to Dorothy. She has Dorothy spinning in circles in Kansas and now here in Oz, with more warnings and threats.

We wonder about all this fuss over the Ruby Slippers. What is so darn important about these fabulously embellished shoes?

The Ruby Slippers represent our Powerful Foundation. And the only way we can stand in and operate from our Soul is when we are grounded, aligned and leading with the Self.

When we operate from the ego we feel small and fearful, or to borrow the words that Dorothy will use later in our story, "meek and mild." It is from the ego that we seek our most basic rights of safety, poise, peace, love and joy by looking outside of the Self. But our true power lies with and is found within the Self.

Energetically speaking the Ruby Slippers represent our foundational first chakra. Our chakras are part of our energy body. They are like energetic managers, directing the flow of our fundamental energy. Most of us cannot physically see them, but we can learn to develop a sense of our chakras simply by learning about them and working with them.

Our first chakra is located at the base of our spine. It is red in color, just like the Ruby Slippers. When we have a well balanced first chakra, we are unshakable; we feel safe and confident. When this chakra is out of balance, we feel ungrounded and unsafe.

As a race, we lived from the first chakra during our "caveman days." Our first chakra is closely connected with survival. In our beginnings we were in a state of constant survival mode; each moment spent finding food, looking for safe shelter, and conking menacing mountain lions over the head in order to avoid their eating us. Sex was devoid of all romantic notions; it was simply a mechanism by which to create more of us, in order for the survival of our race.

When the first chakra is out of balance we live on shaky ground. It is difficult to find our footing and we lack the confidence to lead from a Powerful Foundation; to lead from our Self. We have a tendency to hand our power over to the ego and the ego is not an ideal leader.

The ego is *always* in a state of want, which is both disempowering, as well as exhausting. Leading with the ego keeps us living small lives where we are never truly satisfied. Ego-ic wants are misdirected, as they are wants that exist outside of Self. Even in the want for more peace, the ego will seek peace by trying to create it from the outside in. And, strangely enough, the ego thinks that war is a dandy way of creating peace.

Conversely, when we lead with our Self we are in a state of being and we find the peace within. And when that peace is found within we are in a place where all our needs are met. When peace is found within, it then begins to mirror itself in our outer life; as the outer life is a reflection of our inner world.

We are right now being called to stop leading with the ego and start leading with the Self. We must change the inner; inner thoughts, inner dialogue, inner feelings, and inner emotions. We do this so that we may gain the ability to cultivate peace in our inner world and create that peace in our outer world.

The Wicked Witch is a raging ego, who wants the Ruby Slippers so that she may stay in control and hold onto to the *power*. The last thing she wants is for Dorothy to be able to stand in her Powerful Foundation and be in her true power. Therefore, the Wicked Witch will stop at nothing to get the Ruby Slippers; she will plan, scheme, threaten, terrorize and bully Dorothy. And she does this to keep Dorothy in a constant state of fear; as fearful people are far easier to control.

Great and Powerful Perspective #8: Ego Awareness

We too find ourselves in a constant state of fear. We actively invite fear into our lives on a daily basis. Everyday the TV tells us that we should be afraid, on guard and hyper vigilant; a bomb might go off, a plane might go down, our children may be kidnapped. We look outside of ourselves and willingly hand our power over to a government, a religion, an organization or person, all in exchange for keeping us *safe*.

The reality is that we have the power to be safe; we do not need anything outside of ourselves. We all have a pair of Ruby Slippers; we all have the ability and tools to stand in our Powerful Foundation. We just have to re-acquaint ourselves with them and re-learn how to use them.

And so, we must begin by becoming Aware of those wily egos and how they operate in our lives. You know the ego is running your life if you live in fear at any level. Fear is expressed in many ways; anger, sadness, doubt, worry, lies and more. It is time to become Aware of when you are acting from ego and when you are acting from Self; which acts from the guidance of Soul. For example, if you were a country, you may declare war when acting from ego. When you instead choose peace negotiations you act from Self. We act from ego when we participate in gossip and from Self when we speak positively and with loving intent about others.

You can begin acting more from Self today, try blessing the driver that cuts you off in traffic, give a child your *full* attention, stop proving your point and instead just listen to another's, you do not have to agree with them, just listen.

The Self does not allow negative comments to get under the skin for it is Self-Aware and does not rely on other's opinions. When you act from Self, you are comfortable, at ease, non-questioning, safe and joyful about your actions. Begin acting from the Self and be sure to write about your impressions in your Oz Journal.

Also, begin to cultivate an Awareness of your first chakra. As stated earlier, it is located at the base of your spine; it is your foundation. If you were built on shaky ground, which to varying degrees we all were, then you need to come to a place where you can stand firm.

Use that developing Awareness and inner voice to begin to notice when you do not feel safe. And then pay attention to how you handle it. For example, you may begin to feel unsafe when you are unable to pay your bills. And the way you handle this is by eating. Now you understand that when you feel unsafe, you eat. Eating becomes your outer signal that you are feeling unsafe within, now you have something to work with.

Realize, however, that you may not make these connections right off. But as you put your Awareness on your ego and how it operates in your life, these are exactly the types of connections you will be able to make. You can say to yourself often, "I am safe, I am safe, I am safe." Feel that safety within each of your cells. Each time you do not feel safe, say it, sing it, be it. Write it down over and over again in your Oz Journal. Keep doing this until your inner safety is rock solid and you are always standing in your powerful foundation.

Other helpful first chakra balancers are to listen to *grounding* music like that matched with sounds from nature. Of course, spending time in nature is also ideal. We go entire days without touching nature; we walk on it with shoes and pave over it with cement, as if to keep ourselves apart from it. Each day touch some nature. Before walking in the door of your house, stop and place your hand on a tree, keep a plant at your desk and touch its leaves, decorate your space with natural elements like pinecones and sea shells.

You could also carry a red colored rock or crystal in your pocket, like red garnet or red tiger eye, and

hold it whenever you begin to feel unsafe, allow its
energy to ground you.

Beyond this, know that many energy healers are
familiar with chakras and can balance them for
you. There are also several musical CDs
specifically designed to balance the chakras.
Please see the Resource section at the end of this
book for some places that specialize in healing
music.

Dorothy *had* to go to Oz in order to understand her
ego and its controlling, fear-mongering ways. As
we view things from the Soul's perspective, we
see our ego in a whole new light, or more
appropriately, we see how we have allowed our
ego to take over and lead us into an existence
wrought with fear.

The ego, in and of itself, is not a bad thing. Before
coming to Earth, your Soul chose a personality
and way of being for this Earthly trip; and this is
your ego. As we look out at the sea of
personalities and ways of being it is so enjoyable

to see the creative Earthly expressions of each individual Soul. But as we became denser and less in touch with the Self, the Self seceded in running the show and the ego, the denser part of us, took over. The next thing you know, the personality is at center stage showing off its Earthly souvenirs, wanting to buy more souvenirs and coveting its neighbor's souvenirs.

The realm of the ego is coming to a close and it is for this very reason that the ego is so extremely apparent at this time. Everything that needs to come up for healing is coming up for healing, and we would not know to heal it if it were not so very noticeable.

In our story, the Wicked Witch represents the ultimate of ego rule; she is a sociopath. In our world, sociopaths are not as easy to spot as the Wicked Witch; they do not have green skin, pointy noses or sport black capes. But they are here and they are much more prevalent than you might imagine.

Most of us, when we think of a sociopath, tend to think of serial killers, murderers, and rapists. But know that this represents but a few sectors of the sociopath population. Sociopaths exist in our governments, corporations, and neighborhoods. They are the people we think of as lacking in morality, and this is because they are without conscience. Literally.

The most defining characteristic of a sociopath is their lack of remorse or guilt. They lack the human characteristic that keeps most of us from crossing *the line*. They cross *the line* all the time due to their super ego-centric-ism. To them, it is all about them. How you feel, what you want, what may come to pass as a result of their actions is of no consequence to the sociopath. They are *the show,* it's all about them, and they cannot see beyond their own (green and pointy) nose.

The Wicked Witch of the West displays many sociopathic traits. Upon seeing her sister, dead, crushed under a house, she shows an all together *lack of remorse or guilt, shallow affect, callousness and lack of empathy.* She fails to show any of the emotions we might expect when one's sister has met with demise; there are no tears, no sadness, and no expressions of sentiment or loss.

She asks, "Who killed my sister?" She automatically assumes that killing is exactly what has come to pass. She does not even consider that the falling house may have been the result of an accident or natural disaster.

She displays *conning and manipulative-ness*, as well as *grandiose self worth.* In her attempt to retrieve the Ruby Slippers from Dorothy she states, "I'm the only one that knows how to use them. They're no use to you." Finally, there are threats, or *poor behavioral controls*, as she cackles, "I'll get you, my pretty, and your little dog, too."

What I have italicized in the paragraphs above are items from Dr. Robert Hare's Psychopathy Checklist. (Sociopathy is the term now used. For information on where to obtain the full list, please see the Resources at the end of the book.) Realize that laypeople are not at liberty to actually diagnose; this is to be left up to the psychiatrists. But I found it fascinating and informative none-the-less. You may recognize someone you know in Dr. Hare's list.

There are a lot more sociopaths roaming about then you may know. In her fascinating book, *The Sociopath Next Door*, Martha Stout states right on the cover of the book that "1 in 25 ordinary Americans secretly has no conscience and can do anything at all without feeling guilty." Chilling, isn't it?

This, dear ones, is darkness. To live as human without conscience is the darkest and lowest of vibrations. It is what we may describe as evil.

And as difficult as it may be, we with conscience must be in Gratitude for the alarmingly high and apparent rise of the ego. This is healing at the highest order and we are being called to heal it. If we can succeed in bringing light, to those devoid of all light, we can take back our planet and ensure that indeed the "meek shall inherit the earth" (Psalms 25:8).

As such, when you hear of an atrocity committed by a person of the dark, open your heart. Instead of hate, send love; instead of anger, send light. I have vast amounts of hope that together we can heal the world. It takes a village; the human collective village; we can bring peace to all.

We are being called to Ego Awareness in both ourselves as individuals and in the whole of the human race; for we are being affected in a way that does not serve us in a joyful manner. We are affected and have all been affected by those under this complete ego-ic rule throughout history; and when we bump up against them our own egos rise up in fear, loathing, and judgment.

How are we affected? Consider that one sociopath can harm thousands, as in 9/11. One sociopath can kill millions, as in the genocides we have witnessed again and again. One sociopath can create an abusive work environment, corrupt a government and exert massive destruction on a world scale.

Each day make a list of how you acted from ego and how you acted from Self. Know the ego wants to be right, is concerned with its reputation, is super needy and quite childish. The Self is loving, compassionate, serving and disciplined in action and thought. Keep track of your ego-ic ways as well as your Self evidence in your Oz Journal.

9. The Yellow Brick Road

Since Dorothy has made an enemy of the Wicked Witch, Glinda suggests that she get out of Munchkin Land as quickly as possible. Glinda suggests that Dorothy travel to Emerald City to seek help from the mysterious Great and Wonderful Wizard of Oz.

As she does not have a broomstick on which to fly, Dorothy is going to need to walk to Emerald City. But before Glinda sends her on her way, she reminds her to keep the Ruby Slippers on her feet or she will "be at the mercy of the Wicked Witch of the West." Glinda then kisses Dorothy on the top of the head.

When Dorothy asks how she should start off for Emerald City, Glinda remarks, "It's always best to start at the beginning. And all you have to do is follow the Yellow Brick Road." Glinda turns back into an orb and floats off. The Munchkins then lead Dorothy to a spiral path of orange brick, presumably the Orange Brick Road, and a spiral path of yellow brick, the infamous Yellow Brick Road.

Oz Awareness #9: Our Evolution through Our Chakras

Before we venture down the Yellow Brick Road, let's take a moment to ponder the Orange Brick Road. Orange is the color of our second chakra, which is located just below our belly button. As a race, we evolved from the survival mode of the first chakra once we learned agriculture and farming and began to build our own sturdy shelters. Knowing where our next meal would come from and where we would be later resting our weary heads, freed up some space to begin to ponder, feel and become inspired. This chakra is emotion and creativity. And once we moved into this chakra we ventured into art, music, romance and poetry.

Our story and film, *The Wizard of Oz*, for example is an extremely creative piece. Without the workings of the second chakra, the writers, directors, costume designers and such could not have come together to create this amazing piece of inspirational art. So, we give a nice big healthy nod to the swirly orange second chakra and move onto where we, as a race, now reside. This is in the third chakra.

Our third chakra is symbolized by the Yellow Brick Road; it is, of course, yellow in color. It is located at our solar plexus, which is right above the belly button. It is the core of our will and power. Right now our third chakra is in great need of balancing as we tend to exert our will and power *onto* others and/or willingly *hand over* our will and power to others. As we discussed in the previous chapter, we are not living from our powerful foundation.

We lack the ability to stand fully in our powerful foundation as we are not whole and balanced. This is the goal of journeying down the Yellow Brick Road; to become physically whole in order that we can open ourselves up to balance in mind, spirit and emotion.

And though we can always keep an eye on the goal, we must also be steady on our course and not travel too quickly; for the *journey* is just as important, if not more so, as the goal destination. We must take one step, or one skip, at a time. And we must know that with each step or skip we come closer to standing in our powerful foundation.

Great and Powerful Perspective #9: Chakra Awareness

We touched upon this in the last chapter when we talked about our first chakra which is represented by the Ruby Slippers as our powerful foundation. Now we are moving up the chakra ladder and putting our attention on our second and third chakras.

The second chakra is located below the belly button; it is emotion, creativity, and sexuality. Where the element for the first chakra is Earth, the element for the second chakra is water. You can connect with your second chakra by taking a nice long soak in a bath. During the bath listen to highly creative music like a soothing classical piece, or any music that feels flowing and freeing. Also, put a few drops of citrusy orange essential oil or float super thin orange slices in the bath water. After you bathe, be sure to make notes of any impressions that come to you in your Oz Journal.

Also, bring Awareness to your second chakra by keeping in check with your emotions. Allow yourself to feel your emotions, let them move through and out of your body. Use your breath to move the emotions; sighing, for example, is a great way to move emotion.

Also, you can practice toning; toning is the elongation of a tone or note using your voice along with the breath. Listen to your body and make whatever tones your body calls for you to make. And do not judge yourself. Toning is not the same as singing; you do not need to be a diva or virtuoso performer. Sometimes the tones may in fact be melodic, but other times the tones may be, well, not so melodic. Toning is a fantastic way to move stuck emotions.

By their very nature, emotions are meant to move. Think of the word itself: e-motion. When we swallow our emotions and stuff them deep down inside, they, just like standing water, become stagnant and decay. It is for this reason that stuck emotions create imbalances within our bodies. Remind yourself often that, "I am in the flow" and "I am in harmony and balance." Write down all experiences in your Oz Journal.

The third chakra is located above the belly button and as we mentioned earlier, it is will and power. A third chakra that is in balance does not use will and power to control or force anything on or over any other being. Instead it is a steady balanced way of being, where personal will and power are evidenced from within.

The element of the third chakra is fire and we all know the damage incurred by a fire burning out of control. Since the third chakra is also the center of our ego, we are right now witnessing the damage our raging egos can incur.

A way to use fire energy to balance your third chakra is through, what we call in Kundalini Yoga, "breath of fire." Breath of fire is a powerful rhythmic form of breathing where we breathe rapidly in and out through the nose (see Resources section). It aids in balancing the third chakra, and also purifies the blood, charges the nervous system, detoxifies, and is a healing tonic for your glands.

The third chakra is connected with the energy of our true power, our self-esteem and our Earthly personality. To balance it we must work on our confidence and self-reliance. Try taking on a task that exists outside of your normal realm. Though my husband does most household repairs, when he began to travel with his job I had to take on a lot of these duties. I came to do many repairs on my own, and for those tasks I could not do I went out and found reliable handy people. If you are a procrastinator, and not prone to finishing tasks, now is the time to make a pact to accomplish your tasks! Create a list of what you are to get done and each day do at least one task until they are all done.

Since the color of the third chakra is yellow, carry some citrine or amber with you. Citrine is one of the few crystals that can immediately turn negative energy into positive energy without ever needing to be cleared; carry one in your pocket and ask for it to transmute all negative energy for you. Also, keep some yellow daisies or other yellow flowers at your desk, in your kitchen or on your dining table.

The information and ideas shared with you thus far about your first, second and third chakras are most certainly not the full picture. Please do take some time to look up additional information on the internet, buy a book on chakras or take a chakra class (see Resources at the end of this book). Become intimate with your energy centers and see how balancing them can greatly enhance your life and bring you to a more centered existence.

Our first three chakras represent safety, emotional stability and authentic power. When our Earthly needs are met we are financially secure, we have fresh food to eat, clean water to drink, are comfortable in our own skin and at peace with our personal seats of power; we experience a joyful Earthly existence.

With Chakra Awareness we come to better understand ourselves as energy and we allow our genuine Self to shine forth. This then frees us to live in a place of compassion and love.

Work with these various third chakra exercises and remember to journal about your experiences in your Oz Journal.

In order to bring all of this together, we would be wise to also become intimate with our various expressions. And so we make the trip down the Yellow Brick Road. It is along this road that we bring together all of our expressions. Along the Yellow Brick Road we meet, or re-meet, our Mental (The Scarecrow), Spiritual (Tin Man) and

Emotional (Cowardly Lion) Expressions. And this, along with all the other Oz work we do, will contribute to our becoming whole and strong.

10. The Scarecrow

Dorothy is off to Emerald City to see the Wizard of Oz. She follows along the Yellow Brick Road, which up until now, was a straight shot. She comes to a point where the Yellow Brick Road fans out into three different directions. Dorothy stands perplexed, not sure which way to turn. Then a voice makes a suggestion. She is not sure who has spoken. When Toto begins to bark at the Scarecrow, Dorothy says, "Don't be silly, Toto. Scarecrows don't talk."

But it *is* the Scarecrow talking and once Dorothy gets confirmation of this, they strike up a conversation and she learns that the Scarecrow hasn't got a brain. This makes him feel like a failure and when he finds out that Dorothy is going to Emerald City to see the Wizard, the Scarecrow asks if he can tag along. Maybe the Wizard will see fit to give him a brain. So off they go, seemingly without a thought, they simply start walking down one of the three choices of road, as if they know exactly which way to go.

Along the way, Dorothy and the Scarecrow come across a grove of apple trees. Dorothy begins to pick apples and is surprised when a tree slaps her hand and asks her, "What do you think you're doing?" The Scarecrow then *thinks* of a way to get the apple trees to freely give their apples to them. Cleverly, he taunts the trees, and in turn, the trees are compelled to throw their apples at the Scarecrow and Dorothy. In other words, all the apples they could ever want simply rain down upon them.

Oz Awareness #10: Our Mental Expression

In this scene, we see a real turn of events. When the Scarecrow first talks, Dorothy is unaware that he is doing the talking. Then Toto *speaks* up, and she knows what he is *saying*. Whereas before, Toto would bark away and Dorothy would not understand what he was going on about. For the first time we witness her *hearing* him; she is now hearing her inner voice.

Furthermore, in this scene we are also called to become more aware of our Mental Expression and thoughts. We are being called to pay attention and to bring conscious awareness to what we think and do. We have a tendency to run ourselves in an unconscious manner. We are on auto-pilot; we speak and act in an unconscious manner and are unaware of what goes on in our head or with our thoughts or why we act the way we do.

The Scarecrow represents our Mental Expression. And just like the Scarecrow, we may feel as if we don't have a brain; we are instead filled with a head full of straw.

We do, however, have a brain, a mind and *thoughts*. And it is our thoughts about our selves, others and our world that define who we are, and the lives we live.

It is very easy for us to run on automatic. But now is the time for us to welcome surprise, pay more attention, and understand that the evolutionary changes coming around the bend are going to change everything on every level! When Dorothy goes to grab an apple, only to be slapped in the hand by the tree and questioned about her actions, this is saying to us, "Pay attention, be aware, wake up! All is not as it seems."

Great and Powerful Perspective #10: Thought Awareness

When we have Thought Awareness, we begin to create our world in a conscious manner. Energy follows thought; and everything is energy. Our thoughts create the energy that transforms our outer world into the world in which we actually live. If our lives are not joyful, then our thoughts are not joyful; as our outside world mirrors the thoughts of our inner world. If we are seeking a joyful life, then our thoughts will require an upgrade; we need to think beautiful thoughts that nourish and uplift our lives.

We must realize that our thoughts create, or rather co-create, our world. We are part of an interconnected system and we are all part of the creation wheel. We create independently, but also as part of All That Is.

When we become aware of our Mental Expression and have conscious thoughts, we can make amazing things happen. We think in a way that aligns us with All That Is, and we find that what we need simply comes our way. We do not need to pick the apples, the apples rain down from heaven. This is exactly what happens in the movie when Dorothy is engaged with the Scarecrow, her Mental Expression.

Look around you right now, and see what you are thinking. If you are experiencing anything but joy in any area of your life, then you are thinking thoughts embedded in lack in that area of your life. If you are actually experiencing joy in an area of your life, then your thoughts are aligned with abundance in that particular area.

If we were to each think abundantly, then our world would be abundant in all ways. We know that God thinks abundantly, look at the number of cells in each of our bodies, the number of animal species, the number of stars in the sky, and the number of leaves on all the trees that exist on our Earth. We too would not experience lack in our own lives, nor would we be a party to lack in others, if we were to think abundantly about joyful beauty and peaceful calm. It is when we think abundance, not just for ourselves individually, but for the world, that we will experience abundance. This is not the time to think, "Every man for himself", but "Every being for every being." This is the time of Oneness.

Mental mastery is at hand. We must take the scattered straw essence of our thoughts and create thoughts whirling in love and grace.

Throughout your day, ask yourself, "What is my thought right now?" This is where you start. With each thought, go the extra step and ask, "How does this thought play out in my life?" Ooooooo, here is where we can find answers to some of our most perplexing "Why me?" questions.

Let's say for example that you work with someone that always seems to get promotions, has nice clothes, and is invited to the coolest parties. Every time you see them your thought is, "They get everything, and I get nothing." How does this thought play out in your life? Well, according to your thoughts you get nothing, so therefore, that is what you get – nothing.

Now, yes, we could go around in circles with this, you may be thinking right now, "Well if I got things in the first place, I would never have had this thought in the first place." Suffice it to say that somewhere along the line this thought came into being. Perhaps when you were a child, you had a realization that some other child got something you did not have and upon seeing it, you wanted it. And then you began to notice every time that child got something. You magnified it and began to think that they were getting more than you. You then came up with the thought that you "get nothing." And this thought has been creating who you are and your life ever since. Your energy says to yourself and others, do not give me anything for I am to get nothing.

Your head is full of straw.

Now change the thought, and say, "I have everything I need to get what I want." Practice it, write it down, fake it 'til you make it. Each time you catch yourself in a thought pattern that does not serve you, stop it in its tracks, edit it, and give yourself a do over. Let the Universe and All That Is know that you had a thought that you wish to change and then state your new thought, and state it with fervor!

It may take some time to re-pattern your thoughts, but by continuing to be aware and by practicing thoughts that better serve you, magic will begin to happen. Before you know it, you will think "apple" and you will get "apples!"

Also, keep in mind that it is easier to change your thoughts than to change outer circumstances. Let me share an example from my life with you. I am bald. That is right, I am a bald girl, there is not a bit of hair on my body anywhere. For years and years I spent a great deal of time, money and energy trying to grow back my hair. It was terribly distressing; I felt that not having hair somehow made me less than or wrong or diseased.

At some point, I realized that I was spending too much of everything on growing hair, and it all began to seem pointless and ridiculous. Every blood test, hormone test and the like came up showing a healthy me. And yet, I was so overly obsessed with growing hair.

I then began to have different thoughts; like "I am vibrant" and "I am a unique expression of a healthy person." I came to surrender to God and Soul and realize that I could not see from their higher vantage point. I came to trust that perhaps there is a reason for this bald existence, and that this reason extends beyond what I could perceive at that time. I then decided to accept my hairless self. And I came to a place of gratitude for the gifts that my bald head had brought to me.

It took time, but now my being without hair does not affect my life in a negative way. It is what it is. I no longer spend time seeking out hair healers, buying hair growth supplements, wearing wigs, or contemplating strange light up electric hairbrushes that promise to stimulate hair follicles. I figure that if I can change my thoughts about this, then I can change my thoughts about any area where lack exists. My abundance of lessons, growth and maturity far outweigh my lack of hair. What a grand change in perspective for me, and just maybe, for you.

When we change our inner thoughts to accept what *is* right now, and to be at peace with what *is* right now, we open a door to even more. My willingness to accept baldness opened me to information that transcends my Earthly existence. I understand more fully who I am. I feel that it is in my highest good, for I am in the flow and I am ever present with the *heady* changes that may and do come my way.

One of the ways that you can practice Thought Awareness is to write down your thoughts in your Oz Journal at the end of each day. Go through your day and think about your thoughts for that day, then write them down. After you write down your thoughts, notice which thoughts are uplifting and loving and which are heavy and hurting.

The heavy and hurting thoughts need an upgrade. And you get to choose what the new thoughts will be. Write down these new thoughts; replace the heavy and hurting thoughts with uplifting and loving thoughts.

Then, as you go on with your following days, bring Thought Awareness into play each time you catch yourself hanging out with the heavy and hurting thoughts. Give yourself that do over we talked about earlier! Stop the thoughts, edit them and *re-thought* them with awareness this time. And don't forget to do so with fervor!

Our Mental Expression is a key factor in bringing us to wholeness, but it will not bring us all the way Home. We must continue our journey down the Yellow Brick Road to meet up with the rest of our expressions. Next stop, we meet up with our Spiritual Expression, the Tin Man.

11. The Tin Man

As Dorothy gathers up the apples tossed her way, she comes upon a man made of tin. He is rusty and unable to move. Finding an oilcan, the Scarecrow and Dorothy oil his parts, bringing him from rusty to relief. They tell him he is "perfect" since he can once again move around, but he quickly disagrees. He pounds on his chest to reveal a hollow emptiness, and he asks how can he be perfect without a heart?

Dorothy and the Scarecrow, seeing him in need, ask him to join along in their journey to meet the Wizard; who will surely help the Tin Man to find a heart. But before Dorothy and gang can continue on with their journey, the Wicked Witch shows up and she is not happy. She does not like the fact that Dorothy has found some additional support. She threatens the Scarecrow and the Tin Man; even tossing fireballs at the straw ridden Scarecrow to prove her power.

The Witch does succeed in shaking everyone up a bit, but her actions have an unwanted consequence; at least unwanted as far as the Witch is concerned. Rather than break up the gang, she provides them with a reason to further strengthen their bond; the Scarecrow and the Tin Man become ever more determined to help Dorothy. Their mission to Emerald City has changed from a need to fulfill their personal wants to one that is more altruistic in nature.

To this Dorothy says, "You're the best friends anybody ever had. And it's funny, but I feel as if I've known you all the time." They cannot see how this is possible; they both mention that it simply could not be, as she was not around during either of their creations. But she feels the kinship none the less.

Oz Awareness #11: Our Spiritual Expression

The Tin Man is our Spiritual Expression. In this scene we are reminded that as we become whole and find Oneness, we continually bring our Self forth and the ego begins to move into its proper place. The Scarecrow and the Tin Man declare their devotion to Dorothy and the journey; it is as if they have forgotten any want of personal gain and are working toward the greater good. They are with her no matter what, and they are dedicated to helping her reach the Wizard, despite the Witch's threats.

When Dorothy expresses that she feels as if she has known them all along, we are called to ponder. Our Soul is very aware of our various expressions, but we, in this most physically dense Earth body, have simply forgotten that we are more than what is overtly apparent. In this scene we are called to remembrance.

And for remembrance we are going to need to reacquaint ourselves with our Tin Man, our Spiritual Expression. Our Spiritual Expressions have become stiff and rusty as we have exited in this denser realm. We have come to rely on dogma, religion, hard facts, the consensus view and sensible reality. We have given up our birth right of direct connection to God and the Divine and taken on the words and beliefs of others. We buy into belief systems and willingly follow them, believing that *they know* the way, the secrets, and the truths on what to do in order to get to heaven and reap its promised rewards. We give our power over to some *middle man* thinking that he has the gift to speak to and hear God for us and on our behalf.

But really, we do not need a middle man to tell us what we already know to be true. We may not know it from the consciousness from which we operate at this time, but at the level of our Soul we are very well aware that we have a direct connection to God and All That Is. We have simply forgotten how to connect in this most intimate way.

This connection can be made through our hearts. The Tin Man does not think he has a heart, but he has always had a heart. We also have hearts, though we are doing a splendid job of appearing heartless in many instances. If we truly realized our connection to our own hearts, we would not choose war, hate, crime, and violence. We would not allow the ego to rule with its faux power; and we would not allow our powerful Self to stand in silence.

We have heart. We each have a heart, and our hearts are all connected as a Universal Heart; which is in everything, everywhere, in every dimension and throughout all time. We are being called to connect with the Universal Heart thereby connecting with All That Is; thereby knowing Oneness. Oneness is here now, it has always been here, it just is.

Great and Powerful Perspective #11: Universal Heart Connection

In the last chapter, we talked about our Mental Expression and how we can change our lives by changing our thoughts, which is far easier than changing our outer circumstances.

In our Spiritual Expression, we connect with heart. We are a thinking society, and we place a lot of emphasis on our brains and mental-ness; oftentimes forgetting that our heart, too, is full of incredible and far reaching knowledge.

Begin today to be with your heart. Take some time right now. Sit still, quiet your mind, put your hands at your heart chakra, which is located right in the middle of your chest, and just feel the beat and rhythms of your heart. This may be the most amazing moment of your day. Do this often and always allow yourself to marvel.

As you strengthen your heart connection, begin to allow your heart energy to reach out to others daily. Feel the energy of your heart go out and touch the hearts of others then watch as your life begins to flow to the beat of the Universal Heart.

As you do this practice you will begin to learn the information of ages and wisdom that go beyond this physical realm, it is your connection to your own divinity and to the Divine.

During a workshop I attended, we were invited to go into meditation and connect with our hearts. I found a comfortable place to lie down, put my hands at my heart center and went into meditation. It was in this space that I was told my Seed Soul Name of LayaLuna.

I had never even considered the fact that our Souls have names; that in and of itself brought great expansion to me. During this meditation it was also shared with me that the gift of the Seed Soul Name was like being given a key. This key had the ability to reveal to me all that I had kept hidden from myself. Since this event, I have opened myself to learning more about my being and realizing that I am more than what I see in the mirror.

The information I have since learned was given to me a little bit at a time. I see the knowledge in this; to be given all the information at once would simply not have worked. I would have not been ready. Each bit of information brought me to a new level of consciousness and readied me for ever deeper and more profound information and connection.

Over the years, as I continue to put hands to heart, I have come to a place where I am more connected with my own divinity. As well I have experienced a deep realized connection to my guru, known as Babaji, as well as to my Eternal Family, and to the Beautiful And Loving Divine Beings. They guide me in my life, my writing, my healing work, and they guide me to others who wish to connect with their divinity. During sessions with my clients, I have at times been given the honor of sharing another's Seed Soul Name with them.

Do not be in a hurry or feel that you are some how missing out if you do not know your Seed Soul Name. It takes practice to be able to connect so clearly and quickly with the Divine. But do know that if you are feeing called to know this name, dedicate yourself to heart connection; connect with your heart so that you may better know your Soul, the Divine and All That Is. Allow awareness and connection to the Universal Heart and all will begin to be revealed.

And so, as was suggested earlier, take time to be with your heart. In stillness and quiet, place your hands to your heart and allow your heart to *talk* to you. Ask your heart what it wishes to share with you, what messages it has for you, and if it has any ideas on how you can live your life in a more expanded way. Then make sure to note what you have learned in your Oz Journal.

So far, our journey down the Yellow Brick Road has brought together our Physical, Mental and Spiritual Expressions, but in order to fully begin to express our wholeness we must also bring in our

Emotional Expression. And for this, we must come face to face with a lion.

12. The Cowardly Lion

Our trio soon finds themselves in a dark and creepy forest. The Tin Man shares with Dorothy and The Scarecrow that there is a likelihood that they will come upon lions and tigers and bears, oh my!

They do come upon a lion; he jumps out with his dukes up and ready to fight. Toto, the Inner Voice, sees through the lion's pretend prowess and eggs him on to a chase. When the lion goes after tiny Toto, Dorothy slaps him in the face, bringing him to tears. They discover that this mighty king of the forest is nothing more than a cowardly kitty cat. Seeing that he too is in need, in particular, in need of some courage, Dorothy and gang invite him along to accompany them to see the Wizard.

Oz Awareness #12: Our Emotional Expression

"My life has been simply unbearable," says the Cowardly Lion. And right now, many of us feel the same way. In this scene we are called to muster up at least enough courage to come face to face with our unbearable lives and do something about them.

Notice, that up until this scene, Dorothy's Over the Rainbow adventure has been bright and colorful. Both the Scarecrow and the Tin Man are met in bright light spaces, but the Cowardly Lion is found in the dark, but why?

Because the Cowardly Lion represents our Emotional Expression, and right now, many of our emotions are hidden in a dark place. We have a tendency to hide our emotions deep down inside and avoid them. When they do try to come up for release, we beat them back down with distractions, illusions, absurd behaviors, addictions and rationales.

On top of it, we have no idea what emotions really are or what we are supposed to do with them. Though emotions are a most basic verity of human life, most of us were never taught, nor were we really provided with healthy examples, on how to lead healthy emotional lives.

Like everything, emotions are energy. We classify some emotions as good, like happy or glad; and we classify some emotions as bad, like sad or angry. But it would do us well to view emotions in a far grander and more expansive way. Emotions are gifts that help us to navigate our world and teach us the lessons we need in order to grow, mature and develop.

As we mentioned earlier, e-motions are meant to flow and be in motion. But most of us have become emotional containers, keeping and holding on to emotions, sticking them in our bodies, and allowing them to stagnate within our bodies, as well as in our living and work spaces. We are on an emotional loop that keeps us running the same ole behaviors, the same ole addictions, the same ole this and that over and over again in a maddening cycle of dense contraction, never moving into expansion. As the Cowardly Lion states, we end up in a life that is "simply unbearable."

In order to emerge from this unbearable way of being, we are being called to become Emotional Masters. We are being called to learn to manage our feelings in a healthy way and to cultivate a process by which we allow visitation rights only to emotions.

Great and Powerful Perspective #12: Emotional Mastery

In order to achieve Emotional Mastery we realize that when we are visited by an emotion, we are provided with an opportunity for expansion. Rather than take on the emotion and allow it to set up residence in our body, we are to bring awareness to the emotion. This then allows us to learn from it, process it, and release it into the energy we use to create some form of action.

For example, when we are visited by anger, we must bring awareness to this fact and realize that we feel anger. We allow this fiery emotion to put us into a place of action. Anger says, "Get up and do something." It does not say, "Shove me down into your body and make me stay put." Anger, left in a stagnant state can become depression (anger turned inward) or lead to an out lash that is sure to bring harm to others (anger turned outward). Anger left to stagnate in side can affect our liver and other organs; it creates toxins and other bodily imbalances.

Alternately, when the emotion is allowed to teach us, and put us into a place of action, then it can be properly released into the energy of that action. When the emotion comes to us, we must put our awareness on it and ask, why have you come to visit me, what am I to learn? And when we come to understand the lesson, then we take proper action, which may be anything from hugging someone, to starting a business, to forgiving a parent, to telling a secret. Each lesson is unique.

The emotions that we tend to hang onto are fear based. And when we are fearful, we tend to fall into a place where we either misuse our power or become powerless. The Cowardly Lion shows us both of these states.

Just like the bully on the block or the country with loads of weaponry, the Cowardly Lion uses his growl and mighty stature to spread fear; threatening to punch out anyone who dare stand up to him. The misguided thought being, "I am afraid, so I will make you even more afraid, and then I can be in control." But when slapped in the face, the Cowardly Lion quickly crumbles, revealing the powerlessness underlying his outwardly display of brawn.

You are not at the mercy of your emotions; you have a say in your emotional life. When you think that you cannot "help how you feel" you place yourself squarely in emotional cowardice. When, however, you understand that you are the decisive factor in the role of emotions in your life, and that emotions provide you with an opportunity to learn and grow, then you are moving toward Emotional Mastery.

There are several ways to begin to get the stuck emotions moving. They can be coaxed free through detoxification of the physical body; this may be accomplished with a healer or practitioner who specializes in detoxification. To begin on your own move toward a cleaner diet (no processed foods, instead eat God's food; fruit, veggies, grains), and drink lots of fresh water. You can significantly transform your body and emotional health in one month by eating God's food.

However, I totally understand that many of us have strong emotional ties to our cakes and candies, so it can be challenging. For this reason, to start with, consider adding rather than omitting foods from your diet; each day add in some servings of fruit and vegetables. Move onto omitting the cakes and candies when you are emotionally ready.

Since emotions are energy, great healing can come to you when your energy begins to flow. Various types of exercise are great for moving emotional energy; yoga with its twists and turns, as well as Tai Chi and Qi Gong. I happen to love Kundalini Yoga, which through breath and movement create conditions within the body for healing on all levels.

Pay attention to that body, the areas that are tight and sore are a message to you that emotions are stuck in that place. You can do wonders for yourself by learning to use a foam roller or massage balls designed to help you work out those kinks and knots that have developed in your muscles and tissues.

Or learn how to do some reflexology (see Resources). Treat yourself to a massage; and know that during a massage it is not at all uncommon to feel various emotions and, sometimes, simply begin crying. That is okay; massage therapists know this and should be very gentle with you as the stuck emotions release.

Also, consider visiting with an energy healer or do some energy healing on your own. One of the most amazing forms of self energy healing I have come across is Emotional Freedom Technique or EFT. This has been described as acupuncture without the needles. It is accomplished by tapping on various meridian points while feeling the emotion you wish to release. Great healing can occur quite rapidly. Check out the resources at the end of this book for more information.

One of the ways that you will know you are healing is when you feel the urge to clear and de-clutter your living and work spaces. You will want to free yourself of having too much stuff; you will want to throw out the old in order to make room for the new. Just as your body becomes light-er and freer, you will want the same for your spaces.

You will feel a need to clean out the garage, attic, basement, closets, and allow your spaces to breathe and flow. You will know that major growth has occurred when you no longer have a nostalgic yen to hold onto old love letters, year books, or knick knack mementos from a long ago era.

Intention is also in order. Begin to learn to decipher the intention of the emotion, ask why did it come for a visit? Why did the Universe see fit to send this emotional message to you? How does this emotion enhance your life? And what action(s) are you to take?

The *action* may be to actually move in some way, start something, stop something or be still and just feel. Ask yourself these questions; then provide yourself with the necessary quiet space to allow the answers to come, and as always, be aware. Be sure to write about your experiences in your Oz Journal.

Acknowledge that you are Courageous, not cowardly. You are a Lion and you are on your way to Emotional Mastery. Just by knowing that emotions are packets of love, meant to move you into a more expansive way of being, will bring you into a courageous state.

Emotions are a part of our human experience. To deny this most useful tool, is to deny a most precious gift. Uplift your life from unbearable and thrive on the plane of joy!

We are well on our way to becoming whole. We hop back onto the Yellow Brick Road, now with all of our Expressions (Physical, Mental, Spiritual and Emotional) skipping along, arm in arm, full of optimism and verve.

13. Poppies

As the foursome skips along, the Wicked Witch of the West realizes that she needs to take things up a notch. Her threats have yet to deter Dorothy from her mission to meet the Wizard. She wants those Ruby Slippers; for once she has them she believes her power will be the "greatest in Oz." So, the Witch creates a field of poisonous poppies that lie between the Yellow Brick Road and the entrance to Emerald City. As the foursome cross through the beckoning field, Dorothy becomes fatigued and falls unconscious; Toto too falls asleep in the Poppies as does the Cowardly Lion.

The Scarecrow realizes that the Poppies smell of a Wicked Witch spell, and he and the Tin Man begin to call out for help. Glinda appears in the Heavens; she tenderly waves her magic wand, and an awakening snow falls from the sky.

Dorothy, Toto and the Cowardly Lion are revived and upon awakening they realize that the Tin Man has rusted again, so they quickly begin to oil him back up. Meanwhile, as the Witch watches on she cackles, "Curses. Curses. Somebody always helps that girl."

Oz Awareness #13: Our Great Awakening

This scene is a look at what we are experiencing right now. As we emerge from the third Yellow Brick Road chakra, we come into our fourth chakra, which is the heart. And in our story the heart chakra is represented by Emerald City. The color of the heart chakra is, of course, green; in the case of our story, emerald green. Our heart chakra is most obviously about love and compassion, but it is also about balance, healing and Oneness.

This chakra sets right smack dab in the middle of our seven main chakras; with three chakras on either side of it. We have already discussed the first three chakras. And once these are balanced, they will keep our Earthly physical being humming.

The last three main chakras are located at the base of our throat, at the third eye (between the brows) and at our crown (the top of our head). So the heart chakra sits as the bridge between our physical-ness and our divinity.

As stated before, we are in the midst of an evolutionary process. We are right now emerging from the consciousness and frequency of our Yellow Brick Road chakra and into that of our Emerald City chakra. But most of us are asleep in the poppy fields that lie in between; most of us are under the ego's spell. We can make the choice to snooze away, or we can wake up to our divine nature. And we can be of that divine nature right now! We do not have to wait until we die and thereby release the physical body.

Dorothy, Toto and the Cowardly Lion are the three that fall asleep under the spell. Dorothy, as our Physical Expression, does so to represent the fact that we are currently emerging from our three physically based chakras. Toto falls asleep to remind us that we must wake up to our inner voice and begin to listen to it, for this is how our divine

154

part speaks to us. Finally, the Cowardly Lion, as our Emotional Expression, reminds us that we need to wake up to our emotional life.

If we continue to ignore our emotions, imprisoning them in our physical bodies, we will not be able to fully emerge into our heart chakra; we will stay stuck.

Poppies are used to make morphine; which numbs and dulls. The Poppy Field represents how we have numbed and dulled ourselves from our lives. We actively seek medicines, distractions and addictions that numb and dull us from our emotions and pain; rather than face the emotions and face the pain, both of which provide us with an opportunity to transcend our physical and move into our divinity. And it is our ego that works to put us under this spell, for if we go facing our emotions and pain head on, we will reacquaint ourselves with our power and we will begin to lead more with our Self, our Soul. And our ego, which we have spent many years building up and making stronger, will feel threatened and will in turn threaten us.

Though we may not feel connected to our Soul, it does not make the connection any less true. We cannot remove ourselves from our Soul, the removal is illusion. Some traditions talk of losing parts of our Soul and they speak of going to retrieve those parts in order to make ourselves whole again. We can think of these *lost* parts as life-marks. Just as you use a bookmark to hold your place in the book you are reading, the Soul holds a place in your life (or lives) that awaits healing. When we go back to that place and heal it, it puts a piece of our Soul back into its proper place. As each part returns, we come closer to wholeness. And as each of us comes closer to wholeness, we come closer to Oneness.

In order to see past the illusion, we need to wake up! We must view our pain as part of the grand Earth lesson plan; designed to create growth and maturation in a most rapid and expansive manner. Now is the time to wake up and smell the roses;

get up out of the Poppy Field numb-slumber and re-know truth.

It is the Scarecrow and Tin Man that remain awake in the Poppy Fields. The Scarecrow remains awake because our Mental Expression never sleeps, even when we are sleeping. It is always churning out thoughts and recording our experiences.

The Tin Man, as our Spiritual Expression remains awake until Glinda sends the awakening snow. Then he freezes up again, but why? Here we are given a hint as to who Glinda really is. We know she is amazing; she can come and go in a glowing ball, she is obviously revered by the Munchkins, and the Wicked Witch is unable to ruffle even one feather on Glinda's willowy gown. In this scene that we are provided with an even greater hint as to how awesome Glinda truly is. We are shown that she too is watching over us at all times. The fact that the Tin Man freezes only when she shows up in this moment is to help us to see the Awakening at hand; a Spiritual Awakening.

When Dorothy and the Lion wake up from their poppy nap, they wake up and are fully aware that they have shifted in some glorious way. They are Awakened to and more aware of the Spiritual Expression and its connection to Glinda. They notice the Tin Man right upon Awakening and they immediately work to oil him up again. They are ready to get to Emerald City!

Great and Powerful Perspective #14: Our Spiritual Awakening

As each of us individually wake up we begin to wear down an ever more apparent path *up* to our next evolution; by doing so we make it easier for the rest of us to take the journey.

The Yellow Brick Road ends at a Poppy Field, and it is here that we are at choice; fall asleep and stay asleep; which is choosing to wallow, stay in distraction, and live under the ego-ic realm of fear and powerlessness. Or we can choose to wake up and fully partake in our Spiritual Awakening; we can choose to live a life based in love, truth and simplicity. Meaning that we are loving and truthful in all thought and action, and we choose simplicity in all matters; we stop messing with the outer circumstances and know that these will naturally change once we change our inner being.

We have the choice to wallow or wake up because we have free will. And as difficult as it can be to make our own choices, it is perhaps the most amazingly loving, maturity gaining, Soul growing gift that could ever have been bestowed upon us.

Free will can empower us, for although we are all a part of the tapestry of God, we are at the same time each a unique strand of thread, weaving our own journey. And it is up to us to make the journey, for no one else can make it for us. And though it is up to us, we are forever supported and loved in every step we *make*.

Everything that we have talked about thus far is part of our Spiritual Awakening. By waking up to our various expressions, our journey, and our evolution, we wake up to our divinity. Each feeling, each challenge, each confrontation, each joy, each person, each tree, each everything is there to serve you, your journey and your Spiritual Awakening; just as you are here to serve the Spiritual Awakening of others. Put this perspective into play and see how much more you begin to see. As always, write in your Oz Journal, list your wake up calls, and note how you are Spiritually Awakening!

And when you do so, others will follow.

14: Emerald City

As the foursome makes their way to Emerald City, they do so to the singing of a joyful and optimistic chorus.

Our foursome steps up to the gate to bid it open by ringing the bell. The gate keeper opens a small window demanding to know who rang that bell; the foursome own up to it, having no idea why this is an issue. The gate keeper then provides them with a notice reading, "Bell Out of Order. Please Knock." Fine! They knock.

When the foursome requests an audience with the Wizard of Oz, they are told that no one has ever even seen the Wizard. But when they explain that they have been sent by the Good Witch of the North, Glinda, and that Dorothy is wearing the Ruby Slippers to prove it, well that is "a horse of a different color."
So the doors to Emerald City are opened and a whole new world is revealed; a world of unity, with all its residents wearing gleeful garbs of emerald

green, bright smiling faces, and singing with orchestral flair.

A carriage driver greets them telling them that he can take them "anyplace in the city." The carriage is pulled by a horse that is white. It is only after our foursome hops into the carriage, that the horse begins to turn different colors; purple, then red, then yellow.

The carriage does not take them directly to the Wizard, for before Dorothy and gang are to meet him they are to be tidied up a bit. The Scarecrow is fluffed and re-stuffed, the Tin Man is buffed and shined, Dorothy is given a lovely makeover and the Cowardly Lion is brushed and finished with a bow. They are all feeling good and ready to meet the great and powerful Wizard of Oz.

Oz Awareness #14: Our Fear Ridden Hearts

Our foursome is joyful as they make their way to Emerald City, for they have awakened!

But as they step up to enter Emerald City, they are met with silliness. They ring the bell and are then told that must obey the notice; a notice that is not posted. The gatekeeper then brings out the notice, which informs them to knock as the bell is *out of order.* But the bell does work, and the door was answered, so why are our foursome asked to jump through this ridiculous hoop? Instead of questioning this goofy logic they go along with it and knock at the door.

The gatekeeper is Professor Marvel back in Kansas. He is also the carriage driver and soon to be met Wizard. Here he represents not only distraction and illusion, but what is at the very core of the distractions and illusions; and this is fear.

We knock on the perfectly working bell-ed door for no other reason than that we are told to, and we are fearful that our journeys will be all for naught if we were to do anything else. Since the gatekeeper stands between us and our entrance into Emerald City, and we see no alternative, we knock on the door without question.

Fear keeps us locked in distraction and illusion. And fear is everywhere, just as is the Professor Marvel/gate keeper/carriage driver/Wizard. Fear is in the contracts we sign for our *protection*, the just-in-case insurance we buy, and the security gates that guard our communities. Fear is in addictions, weaponry, hate, anger, jealousy and the un-forgiven. Fear is the celebrity of the newsroom.

Fear is the one who claims to know all, and is the one we turn to when we are scared. We believe him when he says that everything is going to be fine and that we should just go on about our day as if nothing ever happened. And we believe him no matter how hollow the words or how many worry lines streak across his brow.

If he cannot keep us safe, then who can? We cannot keep ourselves safe for the world is a scary place full of loonies and psychos. And we know so, because we are told so, over and over again; on news casts, at metal detectors, in advertising, and at internet fire walls.

Somebody is out there, just waiting to bring our fear to an even greater level, and we will hold on to any sense of safety that we have, even if we have to jump through one hoop after another; even if each hoop was created by the hands of the one who crafts fear like a multi-talented Wizard.

After jumping through the *working-bell-does-not-really-work-hoop*, our foursome states the reason for their visit and this is to see the Wizard of Oz. They are then told that "nobody can see the great Oz." Dorothy explains that she was sent by the Good Witch of the North and that she is wearing the Ruby Slippers to prove it. This information grants their entrance into Emerald City.

When they are met by the carriage driver, they are also met with the next hoop; before seeing the Wizard they must first be tidied up a bit. They also meet the "horse of a different color", which is the color of white. White is the pure and perfect combination of all colors; it is the color and light of the pure Love and Oneness of God.

As soon as the foursome hops into the carriage, however, the horse's coat loses its purity and its colors begin to change. This is because our foursome is still riddled with fear; they do not vibrate to pure Love and Oneness yet. When they enter into Emerald City, the heart chakra, becomes a heart that has been struck with fear.

When fear strikes at our heart, we find ourselves in a state of separative-ness; so the pure colors of the horse begin to *separate*. This scene points to our own feelings of being separate from All That Is. We separate ourselves by building up walls through belief systems, borders, and us vs. them mentality. All of which keeps us set apart from others. We are exclusive; some belong with us and others do not, it all depends on where they live, what they do, how they look, how much money they have and who they worship.

Emerald City represents a place of Love and Oneness. The residents of Emerald City sing the same song and move through life in a unified way. But when our fearful foursome show up on the scene, the Emerald City residents are stricken with fear. This is most evident when the Wicked Witch of the West shows up later, and we will learn more about this in our next chapter.

Fear is the great illusion because in truth, we are always safe in the arms of God.

Great and Powerful Perspective #14: In Love and Oneness We Are Always Safe

We expend a lot of energy keeping that which scares us at bay; we have companies dedicated to building weaponry, security systems and monster-sized bottles of antibacterial gels. We spend extra money to include additional air bags in our cars, buy big life insurance policies, and stock up on super supplements promising to restore us to health.

Please understand, that I am not saying to cancel your insurance, start coughing in people's faces or throw out your medication. If you need these things at this time to help you feel secure, then you absolutely must honor the consciousness from which you currently operate and keep these things in place. But be aware that as you release fear from your heart and replace it with Love and Oneness, you will move toward a place of true security. And you will naturally find yourself questioning those supposed *safety nets* you have set up.

All of this will take a huge change in perspective, and you can begin changing your perspective right now.

Begin by becoming aware of what you are afraid of and how that fear translates into your life. Take a good look at what you buy and who you give your power to in order to feel safe. And then, begin to give your fears to heaven.

My daughter and I practice giving our fears to heaven. She came to this world already awakened to her divine connection. But as an *awake* child in a most dense place, she is often confused by the atrocities of this world. She is highly sensitive and simply cannot comprehend why anyone would want to ever say or do anything mean to her. Most are enamored with her. But fear-laden people, especially fear-laden children, are very threatened by her light and are sometimes doggedly determined to squash her light.

She has definitely experienced what it is like to feel unsafe. For the first part of her life, her brother was a very unsafe person to be around. Then when she began school, she met children that came from unsafe environments, and along with their lunchboxes, they brought their fears into the classroom with them.

I am sure that any of you who have school aged children have experienced the same. There seems to be more disordered children than ever before. Remember, all that needs to be healed is coming up for healing at this time.

Giving your fears to heaven is quite simple, but in order for it to actually work you will have to practice. It may take some time. As soon as you feel fear, perhaps you see something on the news, or you do not have enough money to buy something you need, or rumors about layoffs abound, ask yourself where in your body you feel that fear and ask yourself what it looks like. Then visualize your taking that fear and giving it to heaven; see angels reaching their hands out to you and you handing the fear over to them. Know that the angels will transmute those fears into something positive.

The more you do this the easier it will become. You will become aware of the fear quicker, and you will be able to simply hand it over and be done with it. You will still be caught off guard; I know I am, but as soon as I become aware of the fear, I hand it over. And I know as I do this, the darkness within is released and filled with light.

And just as my daughter has experienced, you too may experience those that wish to squash out your light. I did. I noticed that some people in my life seemed rather miffed at my very existence. They were not conscious of it, but somehow I made them uncomfortable.

I had to learn to understand and see that this was simply their fears coming to the surface. When making profound changes, it changes you at the energetic level. And some people will not like this; they already have you in a box and they have already labeled you. When you emerge from that that box and become difficult to label, they do not know what to do with you. Just stay in love with them and keep your light shining.

As you come to Love and Oneness you will know that you have been safe all along. There was never a time, in any existence you have ever experienced, that you were in danger.

Be sure to write about how fear is currently running in your life in your Oz Journal. Then, as you allow heaven to transmute that fear, make note of the details of this Divine allowance.

15: Surrender, Dorothy

Fear strikes the heart of Emerald City when the Wicked Witch shows up and scrawls her threatening message across its sky, "Surrender, Dorothy."

The Emerald City residents run to the Wizard for advice. But the gatekeeper assures everyone that all is fine, there is nothing to worry about and the Wizard has got "matters well in hand." But as he assures them that all will be well, his face is saying something entirely different. At the end of his assurances he throws in a sigh of "I hope" off to the side.

After the Witch's latest threat, Dorothy and gang are more ready than ever to visit with the Wizard. But they are again turned down. The Scarecrow then says, "But she's Dorothy." The gatekeeper questions her unbelievably, "The Witch's Dorothy?" And this fact makes all the difference, he tells the gang to wait and that he will "announce you at once."

Oz Awareness #15: We Have Surrendered to the Ego

At first, Dorothy and gang were granted entrance into Emerald City due to Dorothy's connection to Glinda and the powerful Ruby Slippers that she wears. Essentially, they were allowed in due to their Divine connection. Now, facing once again the possibility of never seeing that darn Wizard, her ticket in is based on an ego-ic connection, and this is her connection to fear; as she is the "Witch's Dorothy."

Here we see that as the ego becomes more and more threatened, it will meet us with equally as large threats; large enough to be very noticeable, in a great big write-it-in-the-sky kind of way. The ego is working to keep its control and the easiest people to control are those that are fearful; those that are afraid to rock the boat, those that keep quietly to themselves and obey, those that will unquestionably knock on the door versus ring the bell.

And those that are knocking at the door of the ego are us, the fearful. This is perhaps one of the most difficult things for us to admit; we so much wish to be fearless. And we kid ourselves about our supposed fearless-ness. Being fearless is not signing up for parachuting lessons, threatening someone with a bomb or putting a great big *Fearless* bumper sticker on your car; these are rationales, distractions, and illusions.

We have surrendered to our egos and it is apparent in all that we do. Now is the time for Surrender from the level of our Soul. And the Soul does not Surrender to the ego.

Great and Powerful Perspective #15: Surrender to God

Surrendering to God is not a passive act. We do not just lie down and say, "Do with me what you will" and wait around for something to happen. True Surrender is a powerful stance.

When we Surrender to God we are exerting our free will to choose God. We are saying, "I need not worry, or be angry or remain in fear because I know that You are always with me." And not only do we say it, but we *feel it*. True Surrender is when no matter what is going on outside of us, we are blissfully aware that what it looks like and what it actually is are two completely different sides of the coin.

Surrendering to God requires a deep knowing that all is well, even when it does not look like it. All is well because we know that God is at the helm, guiding us, sending us messages, coaxing us to move through each trial and tribulation with grace, knowing that our highest good is guaranteed.

As you cultivate trust in God, Surrender comes naturally. When something *bad* happens, rather than run out and buy something, join something or lock yourself up somewhere, decide to just be with it. Do not ask why this is happening, instead ask what you are to learn from it and know that in that learning you will shift and grow.

Surrender to God looks like this; it is you acting from a higher place, acting from the level of the Soul and being in a place of knowing and trusting that all will come out for your highest good. No matter what that looks like, no matter how insignificant or huge it may feel, no matter how it is judged by others. It is free of excuses and rationales. It is done in the utmost love and care.

I woke up one morning and was told by the Divine to stop wearing my wig. At the time I was wearing a wig because I was fearful of not looking like everyone else. I wanted to fit in and not draw attention to myself. When this suggestion was made to me (I have free will remember, I did not have to do this), I could not possibly imagine why my not wearing a wig was at all important. What good would taking off my wig do for me or anyone else?

Then I heard, "Trust it." So, I stopped wearing the wig that day. I had to run errands; I was going to all sorts of places where people knew me. Most people had no idea I had worn a wig, so they were a bit taken aback when they saw me. I simply told everyone that, "I broke up with my wig." To my surprise, no one said anything horrific, no one seemed put-off by this scalp bearing decision, all were quite fine and supportive. And my scalp was most thankful to be free from its stifling wig covering.

As time went on, I came to realize the necessity of this. It was the beginning of my coming out. It was time for me to re-engage into society and become a more active part of my community. I had hidden for many years due to my exhausting life with my extremely traumatized son. Now was the time to come out and claim the real me. To show what I had learned and what I was learning.

I also came to understand how my baldness served others. When people see me they see a happy person. When they see me over and over again they realize that I truly am an authentically happy person; it is not put on or summoned up as my public face.

And this helps people to begin to open up and question themselves. They may ask: Why is she so happy? Why is she not hiding? Why is she not mad at God? Then, perhaps some of them will turn inward and ask, why am I unhappy? Why am I hiding? Why am I so mad at God? These questions allow them to begin to emerge from their darkness and into the light.

When we truly Surrender to God, we become more aware and in tune with our power. We become aware that losing every bit of hair is an amazing lesson in acceptance and Joy and a vehicle through which we can teach. We become aware that the out of control child we adopted, is a spiritual teacher of the highest honor; sent here to push every single one of our buttons, beckoning us to heal from within and heal it all.

Keep your Oz Journal on hand and write down what you become aware of and how you are beginning to see things from this higher perspective. Know that your ultimate safety is found within Surrender to God. Your Soul never *left* God in the first place, and as you come to this realization in your Earth life, you gradually begin to vibrate at a higher frequency.

16: The Wizard of Oz

As our foursome awaits their announcement to finally see the Wizard and receive their just rewards, the Lion entertains them with a song of courage and words of bravery. As he wraps up his king of the forest tune, out comes the gatekeeper to inform our foursome that the Wizard says to "go away", bringing Dorothy straight to tears.

Dorothy laments about Auntie Em and how she "never appreciated it . . . running away and hurting her feelings." She talks about how Auntie Em is sick and possibly dying and that she is at fault for what has come to pass. This sad story creates an opening in the heart of the gatekeeper, who also had an "Aunt Em", and he finally allows them entrance.

The foursome walks into a grand harrowing hall. They are met with a booming commanding voice that demands that they "Come forward." There is fire and smoke emerging from a great stage, then a large green head appears saying, "I am Oz the great and powerful. Who are you?"

Dorothy answers, "If you please, I am Dorothy, the small and meek. We've come to ask you . . ." But she is quickly cut off, for the Wizard "knows" why they have come.

He knows that the Tin Man has dared to come to him for a Heart, the Scarecrow has "the effrontery to ask for a brain" and the Lion is there for courage. The Lion, so emotionally overloaded, collapses and before Dorothy can make sure that the Wizard knows of her request, she tells him that he should be ashamed for frightening one who has come to him for help.

The Wizard then tells them that he "has every intention of granting" their requests, but first they must prove themselves worthy "by performing a very small task." This "small task" is to bring him the broomstick of the Wicked Witch of the West. The Tin Man says, "But if we do that, we'll have to kill her to get it."

The Wizard of Oz demands they bring him the broomstick and he will, at that time, grant their request. Then he sends them on their way. The Lion, so overcome with fear, runs and leaps out the window.

Oz Awareness #16: Proving Our Worthiness

As we have seen, our foursome has had to jump through one hoop after another in order to see the Wizard. In this scene, the hoop they jump through involves Dorothy crying about her Auntie Em and realizing that she never appreciated what Auntie Em had done for her. We must realize that what we are seeing here is growth; many of us do not understand what our caretakers really did for us until we are much older and caring for our own children. Dorothy is maturing.

Finally, being granted entrance to see the Wizard, they are faced with a much larger hoop to jump through. They are told that their requests will only be granted if they take on the seemingly impossible task of bringing back the broom of the Wicked Witch. And they are told that this is how they will prove their worthiness.

We can all relate. We jump through all sorts of hoops and exhaust ourselves every day to prove our worthiness. Many of us figure we must not be worthy as we are not granted our requests. This is despite the fact that we are constantly working for our bosses, our families, our friends and ourselves to prove we are worthy. Carrots dangle in front of us; all those happy commercial people with their perfect purchases and ownership of happy-making things. We jump through one hoop after another, wanting those things that can make us happy, and in return we get laid off, taken for granted and are expected to just keep at it and not question it.

Through the years we become beaten down and have no time or energy left for rejuvenation. When we are told to better ourselves through exercise and meditation we think to ourselves, "How can I possibly fit this into my day, too? I already have too many obligations. And what good would it do anyway?" As a result, we continue to run in the rat race, chasing after that which always eludes us.

Our once hopeful gleaming skin begins to lose its vigor and vim, our bones turn fragile, our organs grow weary, and we give up on feeling anything as it all hurts anyway. We wake up everyday, hit the repeat button, and remain unrewarded. We lose hope and wonder if God is really going to come through with all those rewards that have been preached and promised to us.

What truly eludes us is the fact that the most amazing awards come through silence and stillness. Not busy-ness. We can be busy, we can be doing things, but we must balance that with calmness and be-ing. It is the ego that keeps us always on the go.

When we are led by the ego we are filled with fear and we will only be able to pop our heads into Emerald City for a quick visit. We will not be able to hang out for long; for we do not vibrate within its high frequency range of Love and Oneness. As soon as that ego shows up, scrawling threatening messages across the sky, we will be escorted out the gate and be asked to jump through another hoop, like bringing in a broomstick, for example.

Great and Powerful Perspective #16: We are Worthy of Heaven

We have a tendency to Wizard-ize God. We see God as a booming voiced male, who is watching our every move, calculating our heaven worthiness, keeping tabs of our sin meters, and tossing pain and trauma our way to see if we can handle it? It is interesting that we have turned God into fear, and it is at the altar of fear that we have come to worship. When we worship at this altar we choose to go to the Wizard to seek our just rewards and we end up doing a whole *hoopin'* bunch more work to prove our worthiness.

Proving our worthiness is tiring and it is full of empty promises. If you are forever proving your worthiness to a Wizard, the rewards will forever elude you.

Instead, you must come to know that you are Worthy of Heaven! There is no need to prove it, as it already is. If you could see from the perspective of the Soul you would know that you are Worthy of Heaven simply by virtue of the fact that you are a child of God. And anyone, including you, who does not think you Worthy of Heaven stands in judgment, and judgment lies in the realm of the fear.

In the bible there is a set of *10 Commandments* that some believe God gave to us as a sort of holy rule book. If we diligently follow these rules, then we will be allowed into Heaven. And God is always watching, like a Santa Claus in the clouds, making a list and checking it twice to find out who is naughty hell bound (not following the 10 Commandments) or nice and Heaven toward (piously suffering and upholding the 10 Commandments).

I am by no means a biblical scholar, and I am not challenging the translations that have been set forth. I cannot speak to the social and acceptable language usage and terms of the time that this particular section of the bible was written. But, what I can do is come from a place in my heart and share with you the God that I have come to know as I have realized my innate Worthiness.

The God I have come to know does not command to me, for I have free will. Instead the God I know commands these 10 promises for me. I do not have to work to keep these commandments; instead I only need know my innate Worthiness. And in the times when I know my Worthiness at every level of my being, I feel Heaven. And I know when I am in Heaven as these commandments beautifully play themselves out before me.

Heaven is mine whenever I choose it to be. I am in Heaven when I am not leading with my ego. I am in Heaven when I am authentic and living from the level of the Soul. I am in Heaven when I am not compelled to covet, steal, bear false witness, or wrongfully use the name of God. I am in Heaven when these commandments are evident in my life.

Know that you and everyone is Worthy of Heaven. Begin to live your life from this knowing, and it will become ever more apparent. In your Oz Journal write down ways in which you judge others and yourself, as well as how others judge you unworthy. Write and think often: "I am Worthy of Heaven for I am of and in God."

17: The Haunted Forest

"I'd turn back if I were you!" This is the warning our foursome comes face to face with upon entering the Haunted Forest. The Scarecrow mentions that he believes there may be spooks about. When the Tin Man calls it silly and says he does not believe in such things, he is carried high up into the air and then dropped back down to the ground.

The ever watchful Wicked Witch then sends out her Flying Monkeys to capture Dorothy and Toto. She says that they may do what they like with the others, but that she wants Dorothy "alive and unharmed." Then she mentions the Ruby Slippers, saying that she wants those "most of all."

The Flying Monkeys do as told, but while they are at it they really mess with the Scarecrow, throwing his straw stuffing in all directions. They then grab Dorothy and Toto and take off back for the Witch's castle.

Dorothy, now being held a captive in the Witch's castle, is threatened again with Toto's demise, unless she hands over the Ruby Slippers. Of course Dorothy is more than willing to just give them up if it will save Toto.

The Witch reaches out her greedy hands to the Ruby Slippers, but instead receives a hefty electrical shock. Not to be had, the Witch ups the threat from Toto's demise to that of Dorothy's. She realizes that the Ruby Slippers will not come off while Dorothy is alive. But before she takes action, she must decide the best way to do it, as "these things must be done delicately or you hurt the spell." With that, Toto takes off in a mad dash and escapes.

Oz Awareness #17: Our Inner Haunted Forest

Just like our foursome, we cannot live in Emerald City until we have faced the spooks in our Haunted Forest. Despite any warnings, be them in the form of a sign, a friendly bit of advice or an all-out fearful driving admonition, it is something that we must do; we must face our *spooks* or fears, or we will remain blind to that which has us spinning in *tornadic* circles.

Before entering the Haunted Forest our foursome comes face to face with a sign warning them to turn back. The ego does not want them snooping around here, for if they come face to face with their fears, then they may overcome their fears and discover their true power.

The Cowardly Lion, as our Emotional Expression, takes the warning sign at face value and turns around to leave. But the Scarecrow and the Tin Man turn him right back around, knowing that this must be done, for to turn back is to give up. Here we see the expressions uplifting from their fears; their love for Dorothy is now stronger than their fears.

When the Scarecrow mentions that he believes there are spooks about, the Tin Man denies it and the Haunted Forest mocks our Spiritual Expression by tossing him up into the air and dropping him back down as if he were nothing but trash.

When the Flying Monkeys arrive on the scene they do a real number on our Mental Expression, making us feel scattered and confused; as if we are all over the place and not centered. In our world, we have many Flying Monkeys; they are terrorists, warped political views, label warnings, and how-to-keep-yourself-safe newscasts. They come at us from all sides, keep us on our toes, and distract us from venturing inside our Inner Haunted Forests.

Flying Monkeys affect the way we live; from the totally ridiculous, like only allowing small bottles of toiletries to be carried on airplanes, to the possibly life altering, like keeping tabs on our neighbors who may be planning malice and destruction.

The Haunted Forest is the domain of our out-of-control ego. And we must go here, for it is in this place that we face what we must release. If we are truly to lead with the Self, we must enter the forest, kick out our controlling ego, and allow the Self to bring the forest back to peace and balance. We will never be able to remain in Emerald City unless we accomplish this task.

And of course we want to live in Emerald City; it is a most enriching place. We have all been there and we have all seen it and felt its heart and compassion. We have seen this in the case of big tragedies, when the world comes together in song and spirit; raising funds to send food, rescuers, clean-up crews and others to rebuild and heal.

When we experience our own personal tragedies, our families gather to lend a hand, our friends pray, our communities come into our living spaces and aid us in healing. We visit Emerald City each time we perform an act of kindness to another or when an act of kindness is performed on our behalf. We even experience Emerald City when we simply witness an act of kindness.

Once we go into our Haunted Forests, we are given the opportunity to understand the fears that drive us; it is here that we can release our dilemma/traumas and free ourselves to live in our true power.

When the ego rules the roost we find ourselves in a world where we rationalize, deny, pretend, avoid, and believe we are less than this and better than that. The ego does not like equality; it wants levels, hierarchy, labels and categories. It wants to be in control and have armies and guards at its disposal.

But, when we live from the Self, we know we are powerful, simply because we are. There is only one way to get to the place of leading with the Self and the first step is to learn to recognize the ego.

Great and Powerful Perspective #17: Facing Our Fears through Ego Awareness

The ego always believes it is *right*. And anyone who does not think like it does, knows what it knows, acts like it acts, dresses like it dresses or worships like it worships is obviously an idiot. The ego diverts us from living our truth by keeping us distracted and preoccupied with addictions, media, busy work, and keeping-up-with-the Joneses' lifestyles.

If we could just learn to sit still and be quiet and listen to our inner voice, then we would come to a deeper wisdom and gain perspectives and thoughts that align us with our Soul and with God. Instead we allow ourselves to be carried along on the wings of the ego and find ourselves imprisoned in an illusory Witch's Castle.

When the Witch threatens Dorothy's inner voice, Toto, she does so to stay in control. She does not want Dorothy listening to anyone but her, and she has got her eye on the prize of Dorothy's powerful foundation; the Ruby Slippers. Believing that with this most precious resource she will gain ultimate power. When the Ruby Slippers shock her, she turns her attention to Dorothy, feeling as if Dorothy is the only thing that stands between her and the Ruby Slippers; if she can kill Dorothy then the slippers will be hers for sure.

Here we see the Witch blinded by faux power. The Witch cannot survive without Dorothy. Our Earthly egos exist because we exist, not visa versa. We are the creators of our own egos and we created them as a way to interface with others and move about on the Earthly plane via personality and traits. Just as we release our bodies when we *die*, we also release our egos. There is no need for such things when we exist as pure Soul.

On some level, the Witch gets this, so she is not going to act rashly and sees that this needs to be done "delicately." However, because she is an ego that is so out of control, she actually believes that she can figure out a way to be the *creation* that destroys the *creator*.

And have our own egos not tried to do the same? We most certainly have. We behave as if we know what God wants, and what God thinks and we make God out to be some big dude wielding wacky schemes and tests through which we must prove victorious in order to obtain heavenly entrance.

Every day we spend vast amounts of energy killing that which has been created; we kill humans, rainforests, animal populations, and spirit. If Thou Shalt Not Kill were a commandment to be obeyed, we have made up a number of clauses, loopholes and exceptions to this rule.

Facing our fears does not have to be some big scary venture. When I speak of facing fears, I am not suggesting that anyone take up bungee jumping or go tell off that noisy neighbor. Instead, we will be entering into our Inner Haunted Forest and foraging out our hidden fears.

It is for this reason that we must allow our inner voice to break free, for it is through intuition that we can really see the fears for what they are and realize that we actually have nothing to fear at all. It is not so much about killing our fears; instead it is coming to understand our ego in order to reclaim Self. When we *get* our ego, we can understand how it operates and consistently reestablish the Self, until ultimately, the Self reigns constantly and consistently.

Our fears have been built upon the foundation of ego. Our true power has been built upon our powerful foundation, which is based in Self and Soul. At first, most of these fears are not obvious, but there are some tell-tale signs that you can use to bring awareness to the spooks currently lurking in your Inner Haunted Forest.

Begin by asking yourself some questions. What am I most opinionated about? What do I feel I must be *right* about? What do I do or say to make myself look better in the eyes of others? How do I view others who do not see the world as I do?

This will give you a glimpse into your ego's workings, better yet *overworkings*, in your life.

Begin to bring awareness to all that you say and do. Is there anything in your life that you are rationalizing about; perhaps in order to make it seem like what you are doing or saying makes sense to yourself? Is there something you do to hide what you are really doing? Are you trying to bamboozle others into thinking you are something that you are not? When you get those little feelings of discomfort, this is your inner voice asking you to take a look at this and realize that it is not in your highest good.

If you feel up to it, and you will need to muster up some courage for this one, perhaps you can ask a dear someone for help. This someone is one in which you have complete trust and is of high integrity. Ask them to share with you, in all honesty and sincerity, "What should I change in my life that would greatly benefit others and myself?" This could be quite ego diminishing, so be ready, and do not lash out at the other person for what they may say. Remember that you asked and by not lashing out you are working toward leading with the Self.

Think carefully about this exercise, as it could be a recipe for disaster if done from the ego. The ego may look at it as a way to find out what another "really thinks about me" and may use it as an opportunity to get in a bunch of "I knew its" and "I told you so's." This will only serve to further ego-ic rule and divert us from facing our fears.

Once you begin to have a feel for ways in which the ego operates in your life, you can then begin to ask, "What am I afraid of and how do my ego-ic behaviors and beliefs reveal my greatest fears?"

Let's take something simple like gossiping; we may rationalize it by saying that it is "all in good fun" or "they wouldn't mind that I am telling you this", but it is not fun for the person being gossiped about, nor may it be fun for others who are subjected to the gossip. Bringing it down to a vibratory level, gossip vibrates low. It does not do

well to speak ill or make fun of others. In reality it
is never in good fun.

This can be very challenging, for it can be
especially easy to gossip about and make fun of
people who you will more than likely never meet,
like celebrities and such. But the energy you put
out can be very harming. And remember, when
you make fun of another you are really just making
fun of that which you recognize in yourself.
Perhaps you have never actually acted upon that
which another has acted upon, but we all have the
potential to act similarly; especially when we are
held in ego control.

We also must consider a perspective change; for
though the ego does get a bad rap, it is at the
same time in perfect order. As we have sunk
lower and lower into density we have at the same
time been in the midst of collecting data and
learning grand lessons. What we learn, God
learns.

By fragmenting into these billions upon billions of expressions, God learns more about Everything. And for our Souls, these grand lessons will ultimately bring us to a world that lies far beyond our density. Literally, to a world that lies in a different dimension all together.

We have sunken deep into density, and now, as we make the conscious and loving choice to emerge from this density, we begin our ascent back into our Self and Soul. The only difference being that we are becoming a more fully mature Soul. We are growing up, as is God.

And so, in the end, we do ourselves no service by participating in and affirming the ego as our leader. Jump on the evolutionary bandwagon, my friends, and ascend into the light. Your Soul awaits.

18: Dorothy Calls for Auntie Em

The Wicked Witch turns over a huge hourglass filled with blood red sand, she tells Dorothy that this sand measures the time she has left to live. She then storms off to plan for Dorothy's demise. Distraught and scared, Dorothy calls out to Auntie Em, who then appears in the Witch's crystal ball. And just as she is calling out for Auntie Em, Auntie Em is calling out for her too. Then Auntie Em's face blurs and in its place appears that of the loud, cackling Wicked Witch.

Oz Awareness #18: Our Auntie Em

In our story Dorothy's caretakers are her Uncle Henry and Auntie Em. And this begs the question, why? Where are Dorothy's real parents? Why is she instead living with her Auntie Em and Uncle Henry? Are her parents still alive or did they befall some fateful accident? We are meant to ponder this, for if we were not then this parentage question would have been satisfied at some point in the story. Instead we are just left hanging.

The answer lies in the un-telling; we must come to know that our parents and/or caregivers are not always going to be there to parent us. At some point, we must parent ourselves.

Whether blessed with doting, loving parents or horrific parenting examples, in the end we all must parent ourselves and do so on many levels. We may not necessarily be responsible for what happened to us in childhood. Nor are we directly responsible for the inherited experiences of our ancestors, whose memories are energetically bound to our cells. But we are responsible for our own healing. And we are responsible for parenting ourselves when our parents or caregivers are unable, or not available, to accomplishing the parental duties on our behalf.

We are in pain, we have been hurt, we have experienced events where mature navigation was unavailable and we were left up to our own devices to figure things out. If we put it all on hold and wait for the parenting to come from somewhere outside of us, we do ourselves a mighty disservice. If we are waiting for our parents to finally live up to their duty or are seeking parenting from a partner, friend or other outside source, then we may be waiting around for a mighty long time.

This is not to say that we should not seek help and support, in fact that is quite advisable. But in the end, we are the ones who must do the healing; we cannot rely on someone else to do it for us.

It is for this reason that Auntie Em and Uncle Henry do not make an appearance in Oz. Everyone else is there; Dorothy, Toto, Almira Gulch, the farmhands, even the wandering mystic. But Auntie Em and Uncle Henry can not be there, for when it comes to becoming whole, it is ultimately up to *our* Dorothy.

Another point we must come to ponder is our ancestral bloodline. We are a product of our bloodline; it does not stop with mom and dad, but reaches out into the lives of aunts, uncles, grandparents and beyond. We must realize that healing the past traumas of our own current life may only take us so far. As we journey to heal our lives, we may at some point come to a *dead* end. And when we get here, we must realize that where the healing ends with our own life, it picks up with the lives of our ancestors. These answers lie in the pasts with which our Souls have touched and intermingled.

I realize that these ideas may not coincide with your current belief system. I am not asking you to do anything but be willing to consider the possibilities; and to not close the door in utter disbelief. If it heals and creates your life more joyous, why not give it a bit of consideration. I can tell you that it has been a huge part of mine and my son's healing.

Realize that just like Dorothy, when we call out for our own Auntie Ems, we end up facing our ego. We face the very part of us that needs the most parenting. Egos mimic the childlike behaviors that are calling for the most parental attention. The ego is all about me and mine, it wants what everyone else has or at least something way better, it scans the horizon for the best toys and trinkets and tries to figure out how to get them, it misbehaves when it does not get its way, it acts from anger and believes that joy is found in things.

The ego is very childlike. Do you want to be lead by a child or by a mature and loving Soul?

Great and Powerful Perspective #18: Responsible Self Parenting

When we become responsible for all of our pasts and for all who have contributed to our being, we then agree to take on the greatest task of healing. And as we heal ourselves on every level, we become truly mature, uncover our power and live in authenticity.

There are several ways to approach this, and I would like to share some ideas and practices that are available to help you. Please do take a look at the Resource section for more information.

You may look into past life regression; I offer this to my clients, and it is astonishing how quickly lives can heal. Sometimes our past life experiences are so profound that we carry them into the life we are currently living; and my oh my, they can certainly wreak havoc on our current existences. Once they are brought into our current consciousness, it is often all that is necessary for release and healing.

Ancestral healing is another area that can be of great help to you. Some of the latest scientific research has revealed that we are not only a product of our genes when it comes to the shape of our feet, blood type and facial expressions, but our genes can also carry energetic patterns created by our ancestors.

This is the study of *epigenetics*, and it speaks to our gene expression; or the way our genes express themselves. This puts a whole new spin on Nature vs. Nurture. For what epigenetics reveals to us is that not only may you inherit great grandmother's dimples, but you may also inherit her loving ways, or as the case may be, her nasty disposition.

Please note that my short explanation of the science of epigenetics is blazingly simplified, and that the scope of this amazing study goes way beyond the offerings of this little book. It is my goal to bring it into your awareness, so that you can begin to understand that our ancestors, and not only the ancestors we know or have known, but those from several generations ago, may pass on a lot more than looks.

Of course, you can always do some ancestral healing on your own. If you have any interest in this, I honor you! This is a huge step in recognizing and being in Oneness.

I can also tell you that when you heal something in your past life or in that of an ancestor's, others will inevitably experience healing. I have worked on ancestral healing and have noticed amazing healing in my bloodline. It is very evident in how my family has come to relate with each other.

Of course, realize that individuals have the option to accept the healing or not, for we all have free will. Also consider that this type of healing is done at the Soul level, so the people affected will, more than likely, not be conscious of the healing, nor of their accepting it or not. So don't expect anyone to be sending you "Thank You" cards, but do expect to begin to see it in the relations, it will be quite evident.

One way would be to call upon your ancestors. Simply begin to have a dialogue with them. They are with you at all times for their memories are held within your very being. While in meditation call upon them for help and healing; ask them to help you heal all that needs to be healed within your bloodline. If there is something specific you want help with, all you need do is ask and hold the intention that they are helping you. They are helping; it may not be noticeable right away, be patient and give it time.

Practice *listening*. This does not necessarily mean that you will hear them talking to you, instead you may receive impressions, feelings, or see images and symbols. Be aware! Messages could be sent to you in several ways; you may notice something on a billboard, feel it in a song, have a certain impression when you see a flower or experience déjà vu. These are all examples of ways in which your ancestors may be *talking* to you, so pay attention.

Another option is to speak Soul to Soul. Have your Soul go speak with those of your ancestors and work it all out on their level. This is also an ideal way to work on past life issues. Before going to bed at night, ask your Soul to help you to heal anything from a past life that is keeping you stuck. Again, you may be specific or you may just let your Soul lead the way. Either way, remember to stay in awareness, so that what needs to come into your consciousness does so and allows for sweet release.

I leave this chapter with something else for you to consider. I know this all may seem strange, if not all together insane, to even imply that you can heal what has happened in a distant past. But we must keep in mind that it is on Earth that we have measurable time and space; the ticking of the clock measures time, distances can be measured in millimeters to miles to light years. But in a realm beyond us, time is not a factor, and neither is space.

God transcends time and space. Numerous theories and studies point to the holographic nature of our universe in which subatomic particles, like electrons for example, can instantaneously communicate with each other no matter the amount of distance between them, even if they are billions of miles apart.

In other words, that which appears to separate them is illusion. Yes! Just as we *appear* separate from each other, but are in realty connected as One. And just as in a hologram, each small part is a reflection of the greater whole. Just as each strand of our DNA is a reflection of us; just as each of us is a reflection of God. Each piece of space is a reflection of the entire Universe, each speck of time is a reflection of the past, present and future. We are at the same time child and parent, parent and child.

What does this reveal to us about our greater reality? It tells us we are timeless and infinite. It asks us to look beyond the limits of the world we see before us and to consider that we can in fact heal beyond our own current lives. We can go to the beyond, via our Soul, to heal something that we only perceive as distant or *no longer*. Expand your awareness, know that this power lies within you; heal you and allow this healing to span out into your past, your future as well as to those of past and future generations.

The Wicked Witch ego may think it can keep us locked in captivity (space) in her castle, and locked into the sands running through her hourglass (time), but when we have the courage to practice Responsible Self Parenting, we move beyond these confines and heal.

In this chapter, we have touched upon some rather mind blowing concepts. One of the quickest ways to shatter your current and limited perceptions is to start to look up information about epigenetics, holographic universe, and check out quantum physics as well. Fascinating stuff! Open your entire being to what scientists and spiritualists are learning about our wholeness.

And, of course, do make notes in your Oz Journal about your healing experiences and the knowledge you are gaining!

19: Toto Escapes

When Toto escapes he runs directly to the Scarecrow, Tin Man and Cowardly Lion. He barks and the Scarecrow recognizes right away that Toto has come to lead them to Dorothy.

Toto leads the trio up a treacherous and rocky mountainside to get to the Witch's castle. Once at the castle the guards, or Winkies, are marching and chanting, "Oh We Um, Eoh Um." The Scarecrow says that he has a plan for getting Dorothy out, and his plan involves them being led by the Cowardly Lion, who first responds in confident talk, then ends in wanting someone to "talk him out of it."

As they move along and watch on, three Winkies come up from behind and attack. There is a scuffle, but our threesome is victorious and they successfully overcome the guards. They then relieve the guards of their uniforms, dress up as Winkies themselves and sneak into the castle.

Toto leads them to the place where Dorothy is being held. To free her, the Tin Man uses his ax to break down the door. The whole gang is back together again.

Oz Awareness #19: Captivity

In this scene we see how the Self is becoming whole. When the Scarecrow understands that Toto has escaped in order to lead them to Dorothy, he too is beginning to hear the inner voice.

We also see how the Mental, Spiritual and Emotional Expressions are gaining strength as they act as One; they act together to overcome the Winkies, successfully sneak into the castle, find Dorothy and free her with the Tin Man's ax.

When we first met the Tin Man he was immobile and rusty. He had been holding up his ax for ages and his arm was quite sore. Now we see him using the axe in the interest of freedom. This asks us to question ourselves. How many *burdens* are we carrying about? How many limitations have we placed upon ourselves thereby keeping us stuck in one place, without the freedom to move into joy? How can we turn our *burdens* into tools of freedom?

We can do this by realizing that every burden is an opportunity to heal, mature and grow. Each time we release a burden, we shift upward, we lighten our load and we come through with greater wisdom.

Also, we must realize that we are responsible for our limitations; we are the reason we are stuck and immobile. By engaging all of our expressions and reaching toward wholeness we begin the process of freeing ourselves.

When the Scarecrow, Tin Man, and Cowardly Lion follow Toto and band together as One to rescue Dorothy, they band together in the spirit of Oneness.

Great and Powerful Perspective #19: True Freedom

No one can free us, as we are already free. Even if held in captivity, we can come to know that we are actually free. Holocaust survivors, and others who have been physically held captive, speak of being able to move into a place of True Freedom. They knew with utter certainty that though their physical body may be held captive, the greater part of them; their mind, spirit and emotions were free.

Note how interesting it is that the Winkies bear an eerie resemblance to the Nazis; devotion to a crazed leader who is bent on power, willing to destroy anything that gets in the way of their twisted plans, is wildly ego-centric, and is without conscience. Their movements, their chants, their uniform all have a Nazi essence and feel.

And the leader of such a regime is completely controlled by ego; is imprisoned by that ego. The Witch, like any other overtly ego-crazed being,

219

mirrors the hold the ego has on them by imprisoning others and obsessing about control over the lives of others.

The faux freedom sold to us as devotion to flag, border, party or person is not True Freedom; it is illusion. At the level of the Soul there is no need for anything that separates. And devotion to flag, border, party or person does just that, it separates. True Freedom reigns in Oneness.

We know we can be in a physical body and still visit Oz through meditation, in our dream world and via our imagination. But perhaps we are on the brink of having greater command over our physical body.

Quantum physics shows us that at a subatomic level, particles and waves appear and disappear. Where do they go? If the subatomic particles and waves that make up everything can wink in and out, then can we not do the same; are we even really here?

Yes and no. We are *here* because we have created this place. Our physical senses, however, only allow us to perceive so much, we have to look deeper, broader, and higher in order to really get what we are *made of*. Perhaps, we only *think* we are physically bound; and this limitation is self-imposed. In True Freedom, we are boundless.

Clients that come to me for past life regression will usually spend some time experiencing themselves as Soul. I believe they are brought to Soul in order to help them remember who they really are and to reacquaint themselves with their True Freedom. Usually the client seems content to just hang out as Soul. From the perspective of the onlooker, it seems boring. Many times they don't see or hear anything. Sometimes they see some lights or colors, but that is about it. The feeling, however, tells the story; they always talk about feeling free and at peace.

Sometimes, I wonder if allowing them to hang out there for the entire session would be the most healing. But as the Physical Expression, who is paying money for the session and later receiving a recording of the session, may be disappointed with a recording of them talking about colors and how peaceful and free they feel. I have found that they very much enjoy learning and hearing themselves talk about their past lives as a farmer, a warrior, or their life in ancient Egypt. So I will usually work to move them along after their Soul experience.

Moving them on, however, is quite often met with a bit of resistance. It's as if they don't want to have to leave that place of Soul beauty *again*.

Whenever you feel as if you are not free, affirm it over and over again; "I am free, I am free, I am free." Write this statement down in your Oz Journal. Post it on notes and hang them up around your house. Remind yourself often that you are in fact free and allow the energy of True Freedom to soak into your being.

20: The Wicked Witch is Dead

Just as Dorothy and friends are about to fully escape they are cornered by the Witch and the Winkies. The Witch could not be more pleased, as she has the whole gang cornered; she can now kill them all as opposed to just one. She decides to begin with the Scarecrow and lights him afire.

Quick thinking Dorothy grabs a bucket and throws water at the Scarecrow to put out the flames. She succeeds in doing so, and does not only save the Scarecrow, but gets a bonus. She also succeeds in melting the Wicked Witch. Down she goes, melting and withering away into nothingness.

The Winkies seem startled at first, but they quickly realize that the reign of terror is over and that they too are free. "Hail to Dorothy, the Wicked Witch is dead." In return for the service, Dorothy asks for the broomstick, which they happily hand over to her.

Oz Awareness #20: Watering Down the Ego

And this is what we are being called to do; we are being called to water down our egos. Thus far, we have talked a great deal about Watering Down the Ego and leading from the level of Soul. We are now going to take it a step further. For the ego has been given so much power, that it is now running the world.

We need to be aware that our collective egos have formed our world and lives and that this creation does not speak to our true power. We are blinded from our truth as we are seeing everything from the perspective of our ego.

When we view from the perspective of ego we are out for numero uno, we are overly concerned with eating, drinking, wearing and driving *impressive* brand names. We are constantly on the go to get more money so we can get more stuff. We may even do things that seem to have a true intent, but that actually serve our ego. If the intent for donating money to churches or charities is done because it gives us a favorable nod from friends and family, then we must realize that though we are feeding the world, we are doing so to also feed our egos. The Soul is not concerned with what others think.

When we view all from the perspective of the Soul, what we do is done in the name of All That Is. We are not concerned with how we look to others, but about our wellness and the wellness of all. We often ask, "How may I serve?" It is from this perspective only that we see, hear, speak and know truth.

Great and Powerful Perspective #20: Hello Soul

When we release the ego from its ruling place and nobly step into Soul, a whole new world opens up to us. As you put your awareness on your ego, you will melt through layers and layers of *awarenesses*. It is completely freeing as each day brings you one step closer to Hello Soul.

The Soul requires nothing as it is in a state of having all that it needs. It may take some time before we can get to living as a Physical Expression at Soul level, but it can be done if we decide it to be. And if we can do this, then things will change immensely! For example, of course you know you can live without a designer hand bag, but what about food and water? Is it possible that we could *feed* our body through Soul and forego food or water? I am confident that one day we could do this and more, but we cannot do so until we live from the consciousness that allows for this.

The media is an ego-ic circus and it is for this reason that I highly recommend releasing it from your life. By *media* I mean prominent newscasts and anything that *sells* to your ego; this includes the selling of fear. When you move away from that which dictates to you what *perfection* is supposed to look like, you begin to find the perfection within. When you move away from that which cajoles you into believing you lack because of what you *do not have* you begin to find authentic abundance. And when you do these things you move away from me to We. You move to Oneness.

Become an ego detective and make notes of how you catch your ego operating in your life. As you put your awareness on it and as you place your intention on Soul, a whole new world begins to open up to you and you will see more than you have ever seen before.

Wake up each morning and say, "Hello, Soul!" Begin to realize this most intimate connection and allow the Soul to take the lead. Be sure to keep notes on your Watering Down the Ego and Hello Soul happenings in your Oz Journal.

21: Man Behind the Curtain

With broomstick in hand our foursome returns to see the Wizard of Oz. They will present the broomstick to him and tell him that the Wicked Witch is dead! But instead of sticking to his promise he puts them off, tells them to come back tomorrow and to not "arouse the wrath of the great and powerful Oz."

Dorothy counters that if he were "really great and powerful you'd keep your promises." To which the Wizard says that they should, "Think yourselves lucky that I'm giving you audience tomorrow instead of twenty years from now."

Meanwhile, Toto is wandering about and comes to reveal a man standing behind a curtain. The true *Wizard* is revealed. He tries to keep his hold on the situation by telling the foursome to not pay any "attention to that man behind the curtain," but its curtains for him as the gig is up.

Dorothy marches right up to him and asks him who he is. Still trying to keep up the image, he honks into the microphone that, "I am the great and powerful Wizard of Oz." But the foursome call him on his folly and he finally admits that "I'm a very good man. I'm just a very bad wizard."

Oz Awareness #21: Wizard Promises

Toto reveals to us the truth. People can say one thing, but do another; do one thing, but mean another. It is our inner voice that can allow us to see through crumbling words and actions and discover true intent. It is our Toto that pulls back the curtains to reveal that all those big powerful words and thundering actions are, well, from just a man. No less or no more than we; just a man, hiding behind fireballs, a booming voice and a big menacing head.

And when the *powerful*, who have promised to keep us safe and have promised to reward us once we've proved our worthiness, turns out to be nothing more than drama induced theatrics, we come to an amazing truth; Wizard Promises are empty promises.

We buy the nice car, then after awhile the distraction of its newness wears off and we realize that we are no different than we were before the car. We diet down to a slim size through sheer will, only to find that we are the same person as before, and before we know it we are eating our way back up the scale again. We marry the person that promises to love us and years later watch them walk out the door because they now love someone else.

All of these are examples of Wizard Promises; empty promises. Words and actions loosely held together as they lack the true intent to make them stick.

Great and Powerful Perspective #21: God Promises Love

There is but One who can promise and keep the promise and this is God. God promises to Love and the promise is delivered. The only thing that stands in the way of this Love is us.

We can choose to be in God's Love or follow the false love presented to us via the ego. We can believe in Wizard Promises; but these promises are cleverly masked by illusions, distractions and fear.

God's Love is real and unconditional. No matter what we do, no matter how our society deems us, no matter what we look like, God Loves us. This type of Love is hard for us to imagine, as we are used to love that is conditional; it must be proven, it is based on our actions and behaviors, bank accounts and lifestyles.

To Love unconditionally takes mastery on all levels. This is not to say that we accept abuse from another or remain in a place where our safety is an issue; for we learn unconditional Love by first loving ourselves. It is from this place that we allow that Love to span out from our energy field and touch the hearts of others.

We do not need to be in the same room as, stay married to, or shower lavish gifts onto another in order to Love another. We must Love ourselves enough to remove ourselves from an *unloving* situation. But when we do so, our intent is that we do so in honor of Self, as well as in honor of the other. We love them, we bid them well, we pray they find their peace and one day take their own journey down the Yellow Brick Road. But there is no need for us to stick around for their abuse.

And how do we come to Love those that are so very difficult to Love? First, we must Love them for no other than they are in and of God. That is it; that right there is reason enough. God is far easier to see in some than in others, but no matter, God is always there.

Next, we must understand that their abusiveness, anger, sadness and the like all stem from fear; which means they are doing the best they can as they operate from a consciousness grounded in that fear. They simply cannot understand why they do what they do and it is scary for them, as well as for those around them. Know that the more extreme and dark the behavior, the greater the depth of fear. And the greater the depth of fear, the greater the fear of change, which keeps them locked into their patterns and behaviors.

Finally, we must accept that we are not equipped with the ultimate vantage point of God. The workings of this world are as mysterious as Oz itself. But we have an open invitation to see some of the behind-the-curtain workings. And in order to see this, we must open ourselves up to those possibilities that we have never considered before.

To better illustrate this I offer you this story. A friend of mine attended a conference. One of the speakers told how at one point in his life, his libido shut off. At the time of this occurrence he was healthy and young.

This person is a gay man, and this happened to him in the 80s, at a time when gay men were proudly claiming their rights of equality. Baffled by his libido loss during a most liberating time, he sought the help of a therapist. It was through therapy that he discovered he had been sexually molested by his father. Over time, through hard work and dedication to spiritual practices, he was able to release the traumas of his past and regain his libido.

All of this makes sense to us; we can see how such things would transpire due to the sexual abuse during his youth. But, here is where things get interesting. Once, while he was in meditation, his father came to him and told him that all of what had transpired was decided and agreed upon before they came to Earth. That, as Souls, they agreed to the occurrences of molestation, so that his libido would be turned off. And though it was during a liberating time, it also coincided with a time that heralded in the AIDS crisis. He knew the truth in the message, and was able to heal at an even more profound level.

I realize that this story may really stir up some chaotic notions, if not anger. It may butt up against deeply held beliefs. I share it as an example of how seeing from a higher vantage point can really open you up and out of existing views and blinding belief systems. If you allow yourself the fresh perspectives that come from the much higher vantage point of your Soul, you allow yourself to open to God's Promise of Love. You allow yourself the willingness to look behind that curtain and see ultimate truth, even when that truth is encircled by what we currently put in the uncomfortable, disturbing, and eerie box.

In the density of Earth, we forget who we truly are and what the greater plan is. We forget that we are most fully expressed as a Soul and are of a divine nature. We forget that we are *just visiting*. We forget that we made decisions before being birthed upon this planet. We forget that we set up our own Earthly education. And we did all of this from the perspective of the Soul; knowing that at the end of our stay on this lovely blue planet, we may emerge a wiser and more mature Soul.

And so, be gentle with yourself and others. Make sure to keep notes about how you are opening up your perspectives and allowing for greater flow of God's Promise of Love.

22: Heroic Rewards

Now, with the Wizard's true identity revealed, he also reveals that he does not have the power to provide anyone with anything that they seek; for they already have that which they seek.

The Scarecrow has a brain and has had a brain all along. What he lacks is the recognition of that brain. So the Wizard presents him with a Diploma in ThD, making him a Doctor of Thinkology. Upon this recognition the Scarecrow awakens to his brain and spouts off an impressive sounding mathematical equation. He is in joy and enraptured.

The Cowardly Lion is told that he too has had what he has been looking for all along; courage. He is simply in a state of confusion and does not believe in his courage, due to the fact that he runs away from danger. He is told that, "You are confusing courage with wisdom." In reality, the Lion is a hero and is thus presented with the Triple Cross;

making him an official member of the Legion of Courage.

Next, The Tin Man is told that he does in fact have a heart. The only thing lacking is a testimonial. He is therefore presented with a time clock heart; giving the Tin Man the ability to see and hear the ticking of his own heart.

And now to Dorothy. She knows that what she wants is not inside the Wizard's "black bag." But before all hope of home is lost, the Wizard reveals that he is "an old Kansas man myself." And that it was "while performing spectacular feats of stratospheric skill" his balloon became lost and found its way to Emerald City, where he was asked to be their Wizard. He just happened to have retained the balloon just in case he needed a "quick getaway" and, well, there is no time like the present. And so he offers to personally escort Dorothy back to her home in Kansas.

Oz Awareness #22: Our Ultimate Truth

Here we are beginning to see everything come together. Once the ego is released (Ding Dong the Witch is Dead) we can fully stand in our true power. We are then able to take off the ego-ic blinders and see and know our Ultimate Truth; that we are in fact brainy beings full of courage and heart.

The Wizard's offer to personally escort Dorothy back to Kansas is symbolic in that it is the release of distraction, illusion, fear and untruths from the Universal Heart. He must leave Emerald City, our heart chakra, in order that the energy of this space be allowed to come into fullness with blessings. And, as revealed by the Tin Man's heart, the time is now.

When the Wizard presents the Tin Man with his heart he says, "A heart is not judged by how much you love, but by how much you are loved by others." At first glance this seems like a totally ridiculous statement. But if we look at it from the standpoint of our Ultimate Truth, we understand that we can judge or determine our living of this Truth through its reflection in the hearts of others. And in order to live our Ultimate Truth we will need to bring the total-ness of our Expressions (Physical, Mental, Spiritual and Emotional) into play.

Great and Powerful Perspective #22: Living Our Ultimate Truth

To emerge into Our Ultimate Truth is a continual upward spiral toward light and love. It requires us to fully live in that which has thus far been presented in this book. We are in Gratitude, Meditative, Forgiving, Aware, and Responsible. We are open to receive the messages of our Inner Voice and are in touch with our infinite Soul. We are committed to living from our Soul and choose to release all that keeps us tied to leading with the ego.

In order to do this we will need to actively engage our Mental Expression and be aware of our thoughts. We will need to embrace our Spiritual Expression and move beyond the boundaries that block our direct connection with God and the Divine. We will need to have great courage as we master our Emotional Expression; thereby moving to a place where outside circumstance no longer dictates our inner emotional life. And finally, we will need to be completely committed to this as we move through our day, our spaces and our lives in our Physical Expressions.

We must come to a place where we love the gift of our body, which is just a twinkling hint of Our Ultimate Truth in Soul.

Living in Our Ultimate Truth is more than self-reflection; it is also ego-ic self-destruction. We destruct the self that has been created through ego in order to come to remembrance and gain authenticity of Soul.

We must give up all our rationales and excuses; we must stop living from the stories that make up our life and keep us locked into a certain way of being or behaving. It is time for us to get a new story.

Just because we cannot even remember a time when we did not smoke, does not mean we are locked into smoking forever. Just because our father berated us constantly and we turned out *just fine*, does not mean that we should do the same to our children. Just because we grew up in an unloving home does not mean that we must also create an unloving home. We need to stop explaining why we are distraught, prone to angry outbursts, addicted and compromising and start being God's child in thought and manner.

Living in Our Ultimate Truth changes everything. When we are truthful we practice what we know to be in alignment with God. When we fail, we forgive ourselves, pick ourselves up and give it another go. As we continue on our path and as we develop new ways, we have the courage to realize when these too must be abandoned for something even better. We are in a state of constant flux and change, while simultaneously at ease and in greater peace.

When we examine the Wizard's statement "A heart is not judged by how much you love, but by how much you are loved by others," we realize that the changes we make will become most evident to us in our physical world. Some of these changes may be deemed positive, but some may be deemed negative.

Know that when we begin to break down our old ways, we are ego-ic self-destructing. As a result, things may not *look* positive. But as we continue to break these parts of our lives down, we are also creating fertile land for new growth to take place. And, of course, if we deem one direction to be the wrong path, we can always take another. And so while being willing to explore and open up doors, also be willing to close some doors and take another path. Be aware and listen to your inner voice.

Be in constant and consistent faith that all is in Divine Order. And be watchful; see how your life begins to unfold right before your very eyes, as the *out with the old and in with the real* makes itself evident on the physical plane. You will notice many changes. Some friendships will end, some acquaintances will fall away, some interests will wane, but in their place will come new friendships, new contacts and new interests that are more in line with you and your higher vibration. Your life will begin to become more joyful and magical.

It is an interesting phenomenon. Be in a state of wonder as you watch the changes take place. Even though some of the things going on may be uncomfortable, and you may at times be doubtful, if you can continue to come back to trust and faith in the process and stay committed, it will all work for the greater good. As you continually work to live in Our Ultimate Truth, you will continually be in a place that allows you freedom of movement and being, and you will find that taking the high road becomes easier and more enjoyable.

This is not the time to do as you always do. Now is the time to consider if what you do is in alignment with ego or in alignment with Soul. This is what you must ask yourself at every turn. If you choose alignment with Soul, then you will be making a choice based in Our Ultimate Truth each and every time, and it will come to be seen in each exquisite moment of your life.

23: Wizard Go Back

The Wizard is now being sent back from whence he came with much fanfare and celebration. He implies that he may be gone for good, and this does not seem to disappoint the residents of Emerald City in the least. In his absence, he is leaving them in the good hands of the brainy Scarecrow, a heart-full Tin Man and a courageous Lion.

Dorothy and Toto are in the balloon with the Wizard, and just as they are about to take off, Toto spots a cat and jumps from the balloon. Dorothy, with barely a moment's thought, hops out of the balloon after Toto. The Scarecrow and Lion let go of the balloon's reigns in order to help her catch Toto and with that the balloon takes off; leaving Dorothy to cry for its return. Alas, the Wizard cannot, as he admits, "I can't, I don't know how it works." So much for his being a balloon expert (it seems this guy is really full of hot air).

Dorothy, in tears, realizes that she may never get home.

Oz Awareness #23: Leap of Faith

When Dorothy jumps from the balloon, she is following her inner voice, she is now in a place where she is so connected with her inner voice that she simply follows it without another thought. This scene represents her Leap of Faith. She is showing us that she puts more credence in her inner voice than in the balloon guy's ability to deliver her safely back home.

Her leaping from the balloon does not fall in line with sensible reality at all. She is finally getting her greatest wish, to return home, and she tosses the whole wish aside in pursuit of Toto. What does this say about our own journey?

We too are being called to take a Leap of Faith. The Leap of Faith is our way of jumping up into a new way of being and living. It is our declaration that we have gained what we need in order to leap forward. We have successfully reacquainted ourselves with our Mental, Spiritual and Emotional Expressions, We are stronger, we are gaining resilience, we are becoming adaptable; we have put our trust in ourselves and can now follow our inner voice easily and effortlessly, knowing that it is exactly the right thing to do.

Great and Powerful Perspective #23: Leaping with Grace

When we take the Leap of Faith, we are going to look awkward, strange, weird and a bit odd to those around us. A Leap looks impulsive; it looks like something that we did not think through. And Faith can look misguided; it can look quite idiotic or silly to our closest friends and family.

We cannot take the Leap of Faith until we have gained the strength to weather the eye rolling, concerned looks and advice that is sure to be presented to us by our fellow human beings.

Taking the Leap of Faith will tend to look like a rather preposterous idea but keep in mind that many a preposterous idea ended up being right on.

The world is round, despite the fact that at one time many believed it was not. The Earth does revolve around the sun despite the fact that it was once considered to be a heretical suggestion. E=mc2 completely changed our view of our world, but it was at first met with barely a passing glance. Eventually, everyone caught up to these idea Leaps and put their Faith in them.

There are the trail blazers, and the trail blazers are taking the Leap of Faith and wearing down a path so that others will eventually be able to follow with ease. To be a trail blazer takes courage; it takes great courage to put Faith in that which does not coincide with the collective perspective and with sensible reality. When a radical new idea hits the scene, many are ready with opinions, points of views and debates, all in an effort to prove that they are *right*.

When I took my Leap of Faith, I was met with resistance. What I was doing looked weird, and it definitely looked wrong. I got sick a lot as I was releasing so many toxins. When stuck emotions are released, so are toxins. Toxins can literally hide out in our bodies, and then as we release them we may feel rather ill for a turn or two. I went through a couple of years of catching everything that came my way. I had a cough that lasted well over a year. At one point I developed a rash that would come and go, sometimes taking over large areas of my body. On top of it, my hair was falling out!

To the outsider this all *looked* very wrong. My family and friends were scratching their heads and thinking, "Why doesn't she just stop this nonsense?" I absolutely did question myself, many times. But mostly I knew, at a very deep level, that what I was doing was important and that what I was doing mattered.

As I continued on this path, I eventually came to find others that were doing as I was doing; finding community with these beautiful people gave me some much needed support. As I gathered with like minded individuals, I met many teachers and was showered with love and guidance.

As I continued along my path, I began to open up to worlds and truths that were way beyond what anyone had ever presented to me before. I began to recognize that this information was coming from a place that lies beyond my most apparent world. This information was coming from Beautiful And Loving Divine beings that were speaking to me and guiding me. Life became way more exciting, and I felt my very being become ever more enlightened.

I came to be able to determine when I was shifting to the next level of consciousness and I learned to be in a state of Grace during these times. If I were to view what was going on from a long ago perspective, I would have felt depressed, off, upset or worried about what was going on. But as I became more whole, as my consciousness expanded, I could instead accept the changes and Leap with Grace.

I came to understand that with each shift came a period of releasing, and I could make it as uncomfortable as I wanted. Or I could choose gratitude, forgiveness, responsibility and accept the changes in a graceful manner. I made it *look* easy. Eventually, it actually became easier. I came to embrace the change, rather than brace against it. I welcomed release, knowing that which was released would make room for more light and love.

You will come to this place. So be ready. Soon you will be Leaping with Grace! And don't forget to write about it in your Oz Journal.

24: Glinda Returns

Dorothy, feeling as if home is never going to happen, is comforted by the Scarecrow, Tin Man and Lion. They tell her that she can stay with them. And though she is very thankful for this, she is sad that she may never get back to Auntie Em, Uncle Henry and the farm, as Oz could "never be like Kansas."

Next, Glinda returns, floating in on a lovely pink orb; she comes with news that Dorothy does not "need help any longer." She has had the power to get back to Kansas all along. The Scarecrow asks why Glinda did not share this most useful bit of information before. "Because," Glinda explains, "she wouldn't have believed me. She had to learn it for herself."

The Tin Man then asks Dorothy what she has learned. Dorothy says that, "it wasn't enough just to want to see Uncle Henry and Auntie Em. And it's that if I ever go looking for my heart's desire again, I won't look any further than my own backyard, because if it isn't there I never really lost it to begin with." "That's all it is," Glinda concurs. And all are amazed how easy this lesson is; why didn't any of them think or feel it before?

And now that Dorothy has learned this great lesson, she also learns that the Ruby Slippers can take her and Toto home in only two seconds! The moment is bittersweet, as she realizes she must now say goodbye. She tearfully says goodbye to the Tin Man, the Lion and finally to the Scarecrow. Ready to go, Dorothy closes her eyes, and Glinda instructs her to tap her heels together three times and think to herself, "There's no place like Home."

Oz Awareness #24: God Awareness

Dorothy represents our Physical Expression. And it is in this scene that she has fully emerged as a being that can celebrate her Soul while also honoring her Physical Expression. This is the challenge of this Earthly existence and our next human evolution.

It is interesting to note that the color of the glowing orb that Glinda arrives in on is pink and remains pink. When she came into Munchkin Land, the color of the ball varied in shade. This difference is due to the fact that now she is landing in Emerald City, and Emerald City represents our heart chakra, which as we learned is green in color.

But, the heart chakra also has streaks of pink in it. Many healers and spiritual teachers have seen and sensed that our chakras are at this time beginning to change in color and even shape. Pink is the color of love and perhaps, as we become more loving and compassionate, our heart chakras will be fully awakened within us and will be of a steady loving pink light.

We have already gathered that Glinda is something awesome, but it is in this scene that we are provided with a fuller sense of who She is. When She arrives, it is obvious that She is revered by the Emerald City residents as they bow in Her presence. And the reason for this is that Glinda is the Divine Mother.

God is both Divine Father *and* Divine Mother. We have forgotten this. Generally speaking we use the word "He" as we gender-ize God. We do this because we have been witness to an age where the masculine energies are most apparent. We are a patriarchal society; and we see this imbalance of rule by men and a testosterone-driven handling of situations via wars and weaponry.

All the while, we are also seeing the feminine energies quietly growing in strength and a balance is beginning to emerge. The fact that so many of our households are run by women, many times exclusively so, points to this fact. We also see more and more women run businesses, as well as more women in our board rooms, on managerial staffs, and at the head of our government offices. I am happy to note that I also know a few courageous men out there that are beginning to fully embrace their feminine side. You go guys!

Notice that the word is *balance*. If one gender energy gains more strength and rule than the other, a state of imbalance inevitably ensues. And God is the perfect balance of the two; the perfect balance of Divine Mother and Divine Father. And so, we are being called to remember and know that God is He and She/She and He. Neither can exist peacefully and in pure love without *balance*; with each other and in each other. Balance is ideal and serves all.

This scene also speaks of our personal responsibility to learn the grandest of lessons; we have had the power all along. We cannot come to know this if we continue to act and live from a place of powerless-ness. If we continue to wallow in our pain and traumas, we will fail to know our power. As we raise our vibrations, we experience our power, but we must be willing to do the work and make it so.

For example, we can hear about miracles, we can read about meditation, we can be told the amazing benefits of yoga and we can attend classes about emotional health. But until we actually experience such things in our own lives, we do not truly know their benefits at our deepest levels. And by not allowing ourselves to open up to such experiences we will continue to be opinionated, defensive, close minded and ego-ically tied to proving that we are *right* and they are *wrong*.

It takes enormous courage to be willing to change perspectives and depart from the familiar. There are some that would rather bungee jump off the highest building on Earth than open themselves up to seeing beyond the density and contractive offerings of their religion, politics, clubs and community.

We all have enormous power; we have just forgotten our power. Before being birthed upon Earth, we knew ourselves as Soul and we had God Awareness. To agree to come here, to completely forget who we really are and take on free will – that, my dear ones, takes an amazing amount of power! And just as God does for us, Glinda also does for Dorothy. Glinda allows Dorothy to come to this remembrance on her own. She would not violate the perfection of free will, which is so lovingly set up to help our Souls to mature and grow and find an even greater power; ultimately to help us to come to God Awareness.

Great and Powerful Perspective #24: God is Us

Mired in density, there are layers upon layers of dimensions, vibrations and frequencies that challenge us to find God, here in this place. God is not easy to see here, because we have distorted views of God. We have others telling us that they have seen God, or talked to God, and sometimes we decide to follow them and allow them to form our view of God. But, really, what does God look like, feel like, sound like?

We do not need to go any further than our own Soul to find out.

As stated before, the challenge of this Earthly existence is to be in a Physical Expression, yet live at the level of the Soul. And that is what this book is all about. For until we do this we will never truly feel at home or know our power.

If we live only in the Physical Expression we deny ourselves the opportunity for wholeness. Alternately, we have a tendency to banish the Physical Expression as a vehicle to carnal and self-indulgent pleasures, all of which lead us straight to what we call sin. We view our Physical Expression as a behemoth with which we are burdened. It needs constant care, cleaning, feeding, exercising and rest. It absolutely does not behave; it gets sick, fat, and wrinkly. Our bodies seem bent on creating pain and dissatisfaction.

When our bodies become diseased or disordered in any way, we have a tendency to fall into fear. Instead, we must understand that what we are actually being given is a message from the body, and in turn being given a most beautiful opportunity to heal. And this healing will not only be done on our own behalf, but on the behalf of others; others that are here now, and those that are from and in various times, dimensions and expressions. All we need to do is to transcend fear and find love; it is in this way that all becomes clear and centered and opens us up to healing.

We can come to a place of honor for our bodies. Our bodies do their best and are constantly working in our favor, no matter how we treat them. We could drastically change the state of our bodies, just by sending them love.

The next time you look in the mirror, rather than noticing how much fat has accumulated on your stomach, or how many wrinkles are spreading across your brow, give your body a Joy Flush. Simply feel Joy coming from the Universe and gathering at the top of your head, this is where you seventh or crown chakra is located.

Feel the Joy enter your crown chakra, and come fully into your head. Next send the Joy to fill the chakra located between your brows, the third eye chakra. Now allow the Joy to enter into your fifth or throat chakra, and continue into the heart chakra and down through all the remaining chakras. Flush your body with Joy and know that you are literally changing your cell structure as you are filling each cell with light and love.

As always, be sure to journal about your experiences, feelings and challenges with this in your Oz Journal. Also, as you do the Joy Flush, be aware of any areas that the joy cannot seem to permeate. This is a block.

You can actually talk to the block. Sit quietly in meditation and ask the block what you are to learn from it. Do this exercise again and again until the block is released. Be patient, these things can take time. Know that the more Joy you send to the block, the easier it will be to Flush out!

As you come to more fully appreciate your Physical Expression, you deepen your love and ability to more fully connect with your Mental, Spiritual and Emotional Expressions. And as you come ever closer to wholeness, you become more

Soul focused and you experience God in an entirely different way.

God is *here* and if you want to see God *here* you must learn to see God in the Physical Expression. You must learn to see God in Everything, Everyone and All That Is. God does not only reside in the man built temple, for God's Temple makes up the entire Universe. God does not only reside in the heart of the gentle person raising money for stranded animals, but God resides in all hearts (and lungs, and kidneys, and baby toes, and each and every cell) of every person. God does not only reside in the white dove, but in the hedgehog and the hyena and the hermit crab. God resides in the stapler, the pine needle, the dog collar and the shard of glass.

GOD is EVERYTHING.

And it is as we open up to this, that we begin to understand that we too are Everything, as we are in and of God. We are One. God is Us.

25: Home

Dorothy lands back in Kansas, waking up to the loving voice of Auntie Em. Auntie Em and Uncle Henry talk as if Dorothy has been *out* for a bit, but that her body has been lying on the bed the whole time. We know that she has really been out and about in the Land of Oz.

All are gathered around her and she points out that "you, and you, and you, and you were there." They too were in Oz; this being the farmhands and Professor Marvel. She insists that she was in a "real truly live place" and though all say they believe her, we know that they see her as a little girl who bumped her head and had a weird dream.

She tells them that all she wanted the whole time she was gone was to come back Home and that she was indeed sent back Home. Then she declares, "Oh Auntie Em, there's no place like Home."

Oz Awareness #25: Home

Home is more than just a place, it is a feeling; a state of being. For many of us, Home is an uneasy feeling, because we do not feel at Home. We feel like we do not belong here, that this life is not what we expected, and we do not fit in.

We feel this way because we come from a place where we are free from the physical constraints of time and space. We go from the expansiveness of Soul and into the constrictive density of physical body; the disparity between the two is huge. No wonder babies come out crying and the birth experience creates such trauma for us. Perhaps as we become more expansive we will see fit to completely change the pregnancy and birth experience in order to more lovingly accommodate the journey from Soul to human body.

Coming from the Home of Soul to the density of Earth is uncomfortable for us. Earth is work and struggle. Yes, there are those happy moments, but at times they seem fleeting and so far and few between. As children we had hope; we believed in the rainbow, we believed we could get over it and experience joy. But as life wore down on us, we began to give up. This life does require struggle, but that is okay, for it is how we gain even more strength.

The key to feeling Home is to reconcile this physical life, along with past lives, lives of our ancestors and our Soul life. If we begin to glimpse the larger picture of our existence, we can begin to feel Home.

Dorothy has landed right back where she started; right in her own backyard. And though the yard, the house, and the rest are the same, for her it is has all changed; because Dorothy herself has changed.

Dorothy has gone to Oz and has come back with a much more expansive understanding of who she is. Dorothy now knows of her true power. She sees all with a fresh new eye, an eye that has turned inward in order to create beauty outward.

Dorothy has connected with the Universal Heart and knows that pure love and joy exist right where she stands. She knows that everything around her, each person and each thing, is a part of her. And all is right in her very own backyard. Right in that place that is like no other; right in the arms and glorious embrace of Home.

Great and Powerful Perspective #25: Imagination

By now, you realize that the Wizard of Oz, in our case the movie version, is a masterful map to Home. It is done so in an imaginative way, it does not write it out for us, but instead provides us with the opportunity to allow it to unfold to us in our own way and time.

As stated previously, Home is a feeling. To truly feel Home you are provided at every moment with the opportunity to reconcile all of you; to reconcile all of your expressions (Physical, Mental, Spiritual and Emotional) and come to Soul in order to see the bigger picture. And like Dorothy, we must go to Oz to do so.

Oz lies in our Imagination. The Imagination is an amazing vehicle through which we can find our path, communicate with the Divine, see our thoughts, create our world and find our Home. We do not need to leave our own backyard to take this journey, but we do need to leave our ego-ic created selves in order to re-member, re-see and re-create our fuller sense of Self, our Soul.

It is through our Imagination that we communicate with that Divine part of Self, and our Eternal Family; those that have known us from our very beginnings, your Eternal Family exists in the beyond, yet is with us at every moment. As well, we can communicate with other Divine Beings and Angels, but we must be willing to go into the Oz of our Imaginations

Though Oz is a Universal adventure, the finer details of the journey are unique to each of us. Just as we are all One, we are also each a unique expression of the One God. Each and every unique journey, too, is a part of God's journey.

You can begin your journey today. You can begin to un-stick yourself from your maddening loops, your habitual energetic patterns and your unconscious ways.   You can embrace your connection to Soul, to God, to All That Is. You can grow the pink streaks of light pulsating in your heart chakra and come to embrace the Universal Heart; expanding your love to embrace all of you, all of humanity, and all beings. You can move into a place where you see yourself as part of a Galactic Community.

No longer do you chalk anything up to "just my imagination." Instead you hug each imaginative packet of information and look into their symbols with the wide eyed wonder of a little girl, ready to leap out of the hot air balloon, and follow her inner voice to find Home.

It is the interplay between Imagination and inner voice that provides you with the language of Oz.

When you close your eyes at night, you receive such communications in your dream world. When you are driving along the road and something makes itself known to you, whether it be a long forgotten memory, a billboard, a bird or a cloud, it is your inner voice asking you to take notice and translate the guidance being provided to you. When you see the same number over and over again, when you hear the same words over and over again, when you feel the same feelings over and over again, it is the Universe calling you to take notice and use your Imagination and inner voice to decipher its codes.

By putting your awareness on your Imagination, you begin to decipher what the symbols, images, and visions mean. You will be guided to find books about numbers, dreams, animal imagery and the like. In the beginning, such tools can prove to be invaluable (please see Resources). I love the internet as a symbol of universal connection where we can find information *we* seek, as opposed to being spoon fed that which a select group wants us to know or become. It is on the World Wide Web that we can find loads of information from those that are also seeking wholeness and looking for Home.

Always connect the symbols you see with the feeling you have about them; many times it is the *feeling* that can guide you in a positive direction. Of course, you can always go to a well respected energy healer or psychic, one that acts with integrity and is well practiced in connecting outside the visible world. These beautiful people can help you to decipher the messages of your Imagination.

As you utilize these supportive vehicles you will begin to gain your own sense of Oz. And as you continue to practice you will re-engage greater connection with Oz, and you will understand everything at a deeper level and from a higher perspective. You will come to more fully know the visible Earthly realm and the invisible Oz empire; you will begin to gain the fuller picture provided to you by your Soul.

And you will be able to reconcile all of you, as One, and find your way Home.

So let that Imagination loose! Commit to writing down your imaginative thoughts in your Oz Journal. Carry your journal with you, and jot down these imaginative gifts as they arise and make themselves known to you. Consider each piece of information as part of a puzzle; one that will eventually create a picture for you. You are creating your picture of Home.

26: The End or New Beginning

The End is never the end in an infinite universe. The End is a New Beginning. And in this New Beginning remember to be kind and gentle with yourself and others. Remember to celebrate each day, no matter what it looks like. This does not have to be hard, or difficult or trying. When you see this adventure through the eyes of the Soul it can become graceful, beautiful and balancing.

Allow your thoughts to change. "This is too hard" becomes "This is easy and effortless." When your ego pops up, simply say "Thank you for the lesson." When you meet up with others who find what you are doing to be strange, weird or misguided, realize that they are seeing through fear-focused lenses.

This work is a challenge, but it need not be a challenge that creates angst, it can be and should be a challenge that creates growth. As we head toward the beginning of a new cycle, most notably marked by December 21, 2012, we must realize that we are at the end of a most physically dense cycle; grounded in our first three chakras. It is hard for us to see this cycle, for unlike the 28 day cycle of the Moon revolving around the Earth, this cycle is thousands upon thousands of years long.

The End of this cycle marks the New Beginning; a cycle that is grounded in love and heart. It is a cycling back to Soul and God Awareness; it is a cycling back to Home. Dorothy went to Oz and told everyone she wanted to go Home and eventually she did. And just like Dorothy, we too can get Home. Dorothy never gave up; sure she had some doubts, and she experienced many challenges, but she also came to find greater wholeness and a sense of purpose. And even though her journey was ripe with confusion and difficulty, I bet if you could ask her, she would not have changed one thing, she would see the perfection in each step.

Here is to Our New Beginning!

Live your new beginning each and everyday by celebrating in your Oz Journal. Glue, glitter, scrapbook, bling and bedazzle your Oz Journal. Allow it to become a living expression of the ever-growing, ever-expanding YOU!

27: Author's Notes

This book is a blessing to us. It has been brought to you through me, via the Beautiful And Loving Divine Beings. I look at myself as a Divine translator; taking the images, symbols and visions given to me and translating them into this written material. I have been writing this book for a rather long time. But it was in this writing that I experienced my own journey Home. The book that I ended up writing was nothing like the one I started writing so many years ago. Looking back, I see that I began with an ego heavy book, but ended up with one that has a whole lotta Soul.

I made the time to connect and learn, then write and edit this book. But the actual information was given to me from a much higher place and I am delighted to have been the one to bring it to you.

I use all of my senses to receive messages and guidance from the Divine. There are but two occasions that I consciously remember where I heard actual talking. Once, while writing the book that precluded this one (and that I eventually erased off my hard drive after realizing it was not the book I was to present to you). In that book, I compared myself to Dorothy and when I did so I heard, "This is your book." I immediately ran out that day, bought The Wizard of Oz on DVD and sat down to watch it. Right away I realized that Dorothy was the Physical Expression, meeting up with her Mental, Spiritual and Emotional Expressions. I also made the chakra connection right off. The rest was to unfold later.

The other time I heard actual talking was one morning, upon waking I heard, "You call me Yah-Weh." Now when I first heard this, I immediately forgot it; perhaps due to the fact that the Power of the moment was simply too much for my physical to take. But three days later, I was in a shopping mall parking lot and as I was entering the mall I passed by a white PT Cruiser with license plates that read Yahweh. I almost fell to my knees right then and there. I was completely struck with remembrance of what had just taken place but a few days earlier. It was in that moment that I knew that God had spoken in a most physically direct manner to me. It was an awesome realization.

Both of these experiences are just a few examples when my consciousness shifted greatly and very noticeably in a short amount of time. Mainly the shifts come gradually, but I have trust and faith that they come as needed and come as I am ready to receive them.

In between these two incidences I woke up to the guidance of the Beautiful And Loving Divine beings. They, along with my beloved guru, Babaji, are who I consider to be the main authors of this book. I came to calling them the Beautiful And Loving Divine beings, because that is how I have come to know them. Imagine my delight that when, about a year or so after realizing them and speaking to them on a daily basis, I came to ponder perhaps giving them an acronym; Beautiful And Loving Divine is quite a mouthful. When I figured the acronym out to be BALD, I giggled with joy. It was true and Divine confirmation that my baldness pointed to my remembrance of who I really am. So fun!

If you believe that people do not change, then change that thought immediately. People do change. I am not the person I was twenty, ten or even five years before the writing of this book. Those that knew me in my days of college, or my days of corporate work or during the first years after adopting my son and giving birth to my daughter, would hardly be able to recognize the person now being presented on this Earthly plane.

I have had my share of addictions, twisted self expression, as well as ways and views thwarted by fear. It has been a joy to transcend from the ego-ic person I spent years creating to the *mostly* Soul lead person I am today. I say mostly because I still do go unconscious at times, I still find my ego popping up (especially when someone says and does anything hurtful to my children, or as the case is with my son, when my child threatens to hurt another). I still find myself wanting things that I really do not need, and I still find fears that have yet to be addressed and released.

But now I realize that this is all part of the human experience. And I realize that I am part of a most amazing time; Our New Beginning.

From this humble book may you find a renewed sense of your Soul. May you find a notebook, and write about your own Oz experiences, growth, maturity and learning.

Whenever you feel stuck, simply pull this book back out, close your eyes and allow your Soul to open you to the exact right page. Read until your inner voice tells you that you have read exactly what you needed to read. Then set the book down, pick yourself up, leap back into Oz and be aware as you continue your journey.

In a sense, you are learning to walk in two different worlds. You will go about your day with one foot in Earth and one foot in Oz. At any given time you may be Somewhere Over the Rainbow, in Munchkin Land, on the Yellow Brick Road, snoozing in the Poppy Fields, captured in the Witch's Castle, having a spa day in Emerald City or anywhere betwixt and between. Wherever you are always honor where you are and always be aware of where you are.

And know, that as you walk on Earth and in Oz, you really are Home. And one day, you will feel Home. You've been there before, now Remember.

~ Namaste ~

The Wizard of Oz Code Resources

The Wizard of Oz on **DVD** is available at several stores and internet sites including:
www.amazon.com www.barnesandnoble.com

Forgiveness:

Jesus says to forgive seventy times seven times in the Bible (Matthew 18: 21 - 22). I learned about this exercise in a workshop I attended, given by Sondra Ray. Sondra has written some amazing books, for more about Sondra Ray and her work, please see www.sondraray.com.

EFT:

You can quickly learn this amazing technique and get that energy moving today. Visit www.emofree.com.

Past Life Regression:

I am a student of Dolores Cannon's method of Past Life Regression. For a practitioner in your area, please refer to her web site at:
www.ozarkmt.com/!students.php

Highly Recommended Books on Healing and Changing Your Perspective:

Hand Reflexology: Key to Perfect Health by Mildred Carter & Tammy Weber

The Promise of Energy Psychology by Donna Eden, David Feinstein and Gary Craig.

Heal Your Body by Louise Hay
Colors and Numbers by Louise Hay

Crystal Therapy by Doreen Virtue
Angel Numbers by Doreen Virtue and Lynnette Brown (numbers talk to me and this book tells me what they are saying!)

The Crystal Bible and *Crystal Prescriptions* by Judy Hall

Essential Reiki by Diane Stein

The Hidden Messages in Water by Masaru Emoto

Life Changing Sounds by Dattatreya Siva Baba (about **Mantras**, see www.sivababa.org)

The Genie in Your Genes by Dawson Church (about **Epigenetics**)

Rock Your World with the Divine Mother: Bringing the Sacred Power of the Divine Mother into Our Lives by Sondra Ray

Reinventing the Body, Resurrecting the Soul by Deepak Chopra

Perfect Health by Deepak Chopra
Ageless Body, Timeless Mind by Deepak Chopra

Secrets of the Lost Mode of Prayer by Gregg Braden
The Spontaneous Healing of Belief by Gregg Braden
The Divine Matrix: Bridging Time, Space, Miracles, and Belief by Gregg Braden
Fractal Time: The Secret of 2012 and a New World Age by Gregg Braden

Wheels of Life by Anodea Judith (best book on **Chakras**!)

The 7 Secrets of Sound Healing by Jonathan Goldman

Books on Reactive Attachment Disorder (RAD):

When Love is Not Enough: A Guide to Parenting Children with RAD – Reactive Attachment Disorder by Nancy L. Thomas

Healing Parents: Helping Wounded Children Learn to Trust & Love by Michael Orlans and Terry M. Levy

Beyond Consequences, Logic and Control; A Love–Based Approach to Helping Children with Severe Behaviors by Heather T. Forbes, LCSW and B. Bryan Post, PhD. LCSW

Sociopath (Psychopath) Information:

The Sociopath Next Door by Martha Stout, PhD

I found Dr. Robert D. Hare, PhD's Psychopathy Checklist on the internet at:
http://www.daniweb.com/forums/thread78319.html

Dr. Hare also has several books including:
Without Conscience: The Disturbing World of the Psychopaths Among Us by Robert D. Hare, PhD
Snakes in Suits: When Psychopaths Go to Work by Paul Babiak and Robert D. Hare, PhD

DVDs:

Mudra: Gestures of Power by Sabrina Mesko

Qi Gong for Cleansing with Daisy Lee Garripoli and Francesco Garripoli

Healing the Luminous Body – The Way of the Shaman with Dr. Alberto Villoldo

For the most amazing **Kundalini Yoga DVDs** see www.raviana.com. Their DVDs also include tutorials on how to do the *breath of fire*. I have most of their DVDs and use them all the time!

For **Yoga DVDs** I recommend any DVDs by Baron Baptiste and Rodney Yee. I also like *Yoga Journal's: Beginning Yoga Step by Step Session 1–3* (3 DVD Set). All can be found at www.amazon.com, as well as at other on line stores.

Meditation, Mantras and Healing CDs/MP3s:

www.meditationdna.com
www.eocinstitute.org
www.hemi–sync.com
www.therelaxationcompany.com
www.soundstrue.com
www.healingsounds.com
www.realmusic.com
www.newearthrecords.com
www.sequoiarecords.com
www.amycamie.com

Other Web Site Recommendations for You:

www.youtube.com – do a search for "meditation" and you will find relaxation meditations, chakra meditations, mandala meditations, and more!

Breath of Fire tutorial from Anmolmehta.com:
http://www.youtube.com/watch?v=zsEZylK8sDA

Keep up with what's new at The Wizard of Oz Code Web site:

www.wizardofozcode.com

Follow *The Wizard of Oz Code Blog* at:

http://michhancock.blogspot.com/

Follow me on Twitter!

www.twitter.com/mich_hancock
(that is mich_hancock, don't forget the underscore mark)

Become a Facebook Friend:

Find me at: http://profile.to/michhancock

Spirit Seeker Magazine:

I am a Writer, Editor and Music Reviewer for this wonderful magazine. Come visit us each month: www.spiritseeker.com.

www.ingramcontent.com/pod-product-compliance
Lightning Source LLC
Chambersburg PA
CBHW031242090426
42742CB00007B/280